Thank you for the support.

FROM
PERSONAL
TO
PURPOSE

FINESSING LIFE'S LESSONS AND TRANSFORMING THEM INTO YOUR TRUE CALLING

MASON
THEE DJ FINESSE
SANTOS

FPTPBook

www.From**Personal**To**Purpose**.com

FROM
PERSONAL
TO
PURPOSE

CONTENTS

FROM
PERSONAL
TO
PURPOSE

ACKNOWLEDGMENTS

As you read this book, know that none of this would have been possible without God. He has blessed me beyond comparison. I give all my success to the One above and thank Him daily for my opportunities. I thank Him for the love and support of my family and closest friends. As I look back on my upbringing, I realize I had, and still have the most amazing family.

I have an older brother Chuck who taught me so much. Without him, I honestly believe I would not be here today. As a spoiled little brother who was quick witted and slick with the tongue, he put me in my place one day. Looking back at that moment, he probably saved my life. He is one of the best people I know.

Although he is three years older, he never once missed an opportunity to show me love, help me, and teach me the ropes. I write this book at 50 and nothing has changed. I will always be his little brother and I love him for all he has done and continues to do. Chuck Santos: This book would not be possible without you.

My mom and dad are the world's greatest parents. They encouraged every damn thing I was interested in. Whether it was playing basketball, football, baseball (which I was horrible at, I might add), playing drums, or becoming a DJ; you name it, they supported without judgment.

I believe their investment in my brother and I is why we are who we are today. By investing their time and unconditional love, they taught us the true meaning of love, hard work, and sacrifice. By traveling they showed us a bigger world. They taught us to follow our dreams no matter if what we loved was unpopular.

Their love and support allowed me to be me. The lessons I learned from my parents I take with me to this day and I believe they've guided me well through life, marriage, parenting, and business. Charles and Rachel Santos, I will forever be grateful, and this book would not be possible without you.

I was blessed to meet a young girl who went to Martin Junior High School and then on to East Providence High School. I'd be lying if I said I didn't always have a thing for her. We dated a bit in high school but when we graduated, she (being a teen mom) stayed local and I went off to college. Never in a million years did I think our paths would cross again to this extent. I guess God had a plan that I couldn't deny. He wanted me to marry my best friend. He wanted me to marry a woman who was beautiful inside and out, and who had a zest for life.

He wanted me to marry a woman who challenged me to be better. He wanted me to marry a woman who had class and amazing style. He wanted me to marry a woman I could laugh with every day. He wanted me to marry a woman who reminded me of my mom and whose parents had the same virtues and values as mine.

Mr. & Mrs. Butler, my in-laws: Thank you for everything. God wanted me to marry a woman whose brother and sister reminded me a lot of my brother. Alex and Zina: Thank you. He wanted me to marry the only woman who had the most amazing 8-year-old daughter.

Jessica Janay Butler: You are the definition of what courage, bravery, openness, kindness, talent, and true beauty look like. You didn't have to let me in, but at eight years old you did, and with the kind of love and gentleness that made the transition into parenting seamless. You made it so easy for me. I am so proud to call you my daughter. There was never any confusion as to who I was to you and with you. You let me wear so many hats when it came to your needs.

You may not know it, but you taught me how to be a dad and prepared me for fatherhood. Before you, I planned to emulate my parents. With you, I became a dad for the first time. For that I love you and thank you! I remember saying I wanted a biological son and daughter but then I quickly realized God gave me you and you were the only daughter I ever needed! I love you and this book would not be possible without you.

God wanted me to marry a woman who would give me the son that would lift my spirits to new heights. Every day I wake up and thank God for you, Jarron Christopher Santos, aka "JC." You are everything a father could have ever asked for in a son. You are so well-spoken, handsome, funny, stylish, loving, and extremely talented. I don't know how your heart fits in your chest because it's so big.

Although you are amazing at playing basketball, that does not define you. It's just one more thing you do extremely well. They say we are twins in everything we do and if that is the case, I am blessed beyond words. They also say there is no greater bond than that of a father and son. That is a complete understatement. I know our bond to be truer than anything I've ever known. JC, you have made me a better man, and as I watch you grow, you continue to help me become a better father. This book would not be possible without you.

God wanted me to marry a woman who wasn't afraid

to feed this celebrity DJ some humble pie whenever she felt he needed a slice. Tina Butler, now Mrs. Santos, you are my rock. You are the glue that holds our family together and I will love you until the end of time. This book would not be possible without you.

I tried a lot of things. I've had some failures and some successes, but two passions stuck: Basketball and music. I was the black sheep of my family. Not in the context you may be thinking. I didn't feel like an outcast or feel as though I didn't fit in. Conversely, I stood out because I was "Hip-Hop." I looked and sounded different. I had a swagger about me the culture gave to those who were real. It didn't matter that I was from Rhode Island.

Although I had seen, heard and dabbled in Hip Hop here in Rhode Island, my truest introduction came straight from the New York borough of Brooklyn when I met Masta Ace at the University of Rhode Island in 1987. If you don't know the name Masta Ace, I would advise you to Google him. He is literally a hip-hop legend from the legendary Juice Crew (Marly Marl, Big Daddy Kane, Kool G-Rap, Craig G, Roxanne Shante).

His discography is second to none. He has never wavered from hip-hop and is truly in a lane of his own. Ace literally showed me real hip-hop by staying true to the culture in every sense of the word. No selling out! Being different and original is how he has remained a hip-hop legend. I'm not sure he understands the level of respect I have for him as an artist and even more as a person.

When he introduced me to Hip-Hop, I loved everything about her and everything she stood for. I loved how she walked and talked. She had a style all of her own and I was fixated on it. She opened my eyes and introduced me to a whole new world. She was street, hood, gritty, and educated all in one. Damn, that was sexy to me! Everything that came out of her mouth was real and when she spoke, she had an uncanny way of moving people to action.

I stopped counting the amount of times I went to see her in New York. I quickly realized that's where she was most comfortable. Others were trying to date her, but she saw through them quickly. It's funny though; she had a way of attracting corporate America. She was insatiable and truly the one girl the world wanted to date and marry the minute they saw her. It saddened me when she started dating corporate America. I guess the allure was too much. She was unable to see the toxic nature of the relationship. In my opinion, she stayed in it way too long.

It wasn't long before the relationship became abusive and corporate America started pimping her to the highest bidder. I couldn't stand to see her like that. I did my best to keep her true to herself, but I was no match for the bells and whistles. She ultimately fell victim to the money, bright lights, glamour, and glitz. She spun out of control and started dating everyone. To me it was an unhealthy relationship because not everyone respected her.

As I looked at her I couldn't help but notice she wasn't herself. It was hard seeing her in that light. How can something so beautiful begin to look so unattractive? At that point I decided to walk away. To this day it makes me sad when I think about what happened to her. At least I can say I helped introduce her to Rhode Island and take her to new heights. I loved her when she was real and authentic. To real Hip-Hop and my man Masta Ace: This book would not be possible without you.

Jonathan Rosales: Thank you for your friendship. It's amazing how you can meet a 24-year-old later in life who inspires you to reach your fullest potential. You listened to my story, and by doing so, you encouraged me to write these words. Your inspiration helped me to believe becoming a published author was possible. Thank you for sharing your knowledge, wisdom, time, and resources. Without you, this book would not be possible.

Max Lora: You have been one of my biggest inspirations in such a short period of time. Before you, I had no idea what mentorship looked and sounded like. You showed up in the nick of time. You thought highly enough of me to invest in me. You showed me the value of personal development. You showed me the value of reading content that would help me become a more balanced person. You challenged me daily to become a better leader. You helped me push through the fear that was holding me back. You showed me through your selfless actions what a servant leader looks like. I will follow you to the end of the earth, my brother. Thank you for showing up in our lives. This book would not be possible without you.

To my aunts, uncles, and cousins (too many to mention): Santos, Hazard, Spiva, Delves, Perry, and Bourne... Thank you for helping to mold me, love me, and for playing a huge role in creating the foundation I stand strong on today. They say it takes a village to raise a child. From Wiggins Village to the village of Peacedale, you've had your hand on me this entire time and I love you all.

It's said if you can call one person a true friend, you are lucky. If that statement is true, then I am blessed beyond measure. From elementary to college, I have groups of friends from different chapters in my life who have become family. From East Providence to University of Rhode Island to Rhode Island College, you are my day ones and we will forever be connected. There are too many of you to mention but know the role you continue to play in my life and the life of my family is felt, appreciated, respected, admired and loved.

FROM
PERSONAL
TO
PURPOSE

FOREWORD

What would you do if you wanted to impact the world around you in a way that said, "Hey! I was here and I mattered"? What if you wanted to motivate people, especially those closest to you; how would you do it? If it were up to me I would probably write a verse or a song or create an entire body of music to get my message across. But not everyone can create music.

Buried in chapters full of deep reflection, Mason Santos shares his thoughts about success, motivation, and determination with his readers while giving a revealing account of his upbringing in East Providence, Rhode Island. These writings inspired me to stare directly at my own life and think deeply about what motivates me, the impact I may have had on the people in my life and more importantly the impact those people had on me.

Looking back on my 30 plus year career in the music business, I realize that I am blessed. I say that not just because of the opportunities and experiences hip hop music has afforded me, but also because of the true freedom of expression my music has given me. Through the songs I have written during my career I have been able to share my life's story with the world. Fans who live on the other side of the world know the names of my close family members and have an understanding of what it was like growing up to eventually become the recording artist known as Masta Ace.

I had never given it much thought, but it's clear to me now that perhaps every person wants their life's story to be known. But if you don't rap or sing, how do you share it? When you've looked the angel of death directly in the eye without blinking, you find a way. The idea that you could leave this life without the world having the opportunity to know your story can be a serious motivator. I believe it motivated my friend Mason to write this book.

When I was a young kid growing up in Brooklyn, NY I would often go places with my moms, usually on the subway or the bus. She was like a people magnet. If she saw someone who looked confused or lost she would jump into action, subway map in hand. "Where you tryin' to get to? You need some help?" Within minutes of meeting these people she would be laughing with them and sometimes even exchanging phone numbers with the promise of hanging out one day. That always annoyed me.

Coming up in Brownsville, one of most notoriously rough neighborhoods in the borough of Brooklyn, the distrust of strangers and new people was ingrained in me. I think it is a New York thing. I never let people get too close and always wore a permanent frown on my face. That was my way of letting the world know that I wasn't approachable. But not my moms. She shared her friendly, outgoing personality and her vast knowledge of the New York City subway system with all those willing to engage in some small unsolicited talk. Her personality was a gift, one I did not appreciate at the time.

I never realized how much of that had rubbed off on me until I got older. At the beginning of my senior year (1987) at The University of Rhode Island, I was at the beginning of a career path that wasn't evident to me at the time. I was a Marketing major carrying a 3.0 GPA and looking to get a job at Young & Rubicam upon graduating. My sights were set on becoming an advertising executive and making an impact on television through the commercials I would eventually write. However, I had spent the previous summer recording music at the home studio of one of Hip Hop's most renowned producers, Marley Marl.

Little did I know, winning a rap contest at a skating rink

over the Christmas break of my sophomore year would set me on a course that would change my life forever. I had a cassette tape of the contest that I would sometimes play for people who gathered in my dorm room. Eventually I let a few close friends make copies of the tape to alleviate the traffic in my room. I guess I developed a bit of a reputation on campus because of that tape and the freestyles I was laying down at the school radio station (WRIU).

Mason was one of those friends. At URI he was only a freshman, but I could immediately see he had a genuine interest in this burgeoning culture called Hip Hop. He heard about me dropping rap freestyles at the school station (WRIU) and wanted to be down with all of it. He found his way past the unapproachable frown I wore around campus and pretty quickly we became cool. He even stood in as one of my backup dancers at a talent/fashion show I performed in that year.

After I graduated in 1988, the first record I was a part of was released commercially. I was back in Brooklyn and living with my mother. I decided to go full steam ahead into music and even though Mason was still in school, he was determined to go along for the ride. I don't know how many times he drove up to New York when there was a three-day weekend, but in his mind he was destined to be a card-carrying member of the Hip Hop movement. I had no problem showing him the ropes and taking him around to different events and parties. I knew he would eventually make his own way – which he did, but I was happy to be one of the people to help him reach his destination. After all, it's what my mother would have done.

At my mother's funeral in 2005, I sat there as an endless number of people came up to the microphone at the crowded church to share their personal testimonials about how she had touched their lives. Many of them talked about first meeting her and how it felt like they had been friends forever after only knowing her for a short time. These were co-workers, neighbors and members of her church who felt compelled to share these personal stories about how my mom was connected to them in some small way. In many of the speeches these people, who were strangers to me, considered my mother to be their best friend. I don't think she truly realized how much she had profoundly touched people's lives. My mom was just doing what came naturally… being herself.

So, how do we tell the people in our lives how they have impacted us? Instead of waiting for the funeral we could send them a "Thank You" card and write a few words inside. But those cards don't usually offer a sufficient enough writing area to accommodate all we need to say. We could send them a long text message but that seems far too impersonal. Besides, most people hate seeing giant text bubbles full of huge paragraphs on their phones. We could call them on the phone, but those conversations inevitably get sidetracked into the latest headlines or a recounting of one's difficult day at work.

Because I have music, I would write a song, or even a whole album. But my friend has chosen to tell his story to the world through this book and simultaneously thank the people who have impacted his life. What a great way to exercise his self-expression. Many of the people he introduces in this book will feel familiar to you. They'll remind you of someone in your life. I believe this book will inspire many ordinary folks to tell their own stories. After all, we all have a story worth telling and Mason is no exception.

- Masta Ace

FROM PERSONAL TO PURPOSE

PREFACE

What do you believe? What guides your thoughts and ideas? What are your goals? What kind of man or woman are you? Who do you aspire to be and lastly, what's holding you back from living the life of your dreams?

Who we are and how we move through life – whether we are successful or not in business, sports, relationships, or practically anything – I believe is a direct connection to our life experiences. These experiences in turn help shape our thoughts. The people we meet and the places we live can have a profound effect on how we think, act, and react.

One of my mentors has a philosophy I've adopted. I believe if you can grasp this concept, life will be much more fulfilling. He says life is 10 percent of what happens to you and 90 percent of how you respond to what happens. The things we see, hear, and feel creates an ethical code, a set of morals, and a belief system we use to make decisions along our journey. Our environment, the experiences we have, and our responses to these experiences shape our reality and the perception of the world we live in.

As I write this book, I am doing so at the tender age of 50. I have lived longer than some and less than others. I've had some amazing experiences that have taken me all over the world. In my life there have been successes and continued learning.

My intention as I write this book is to reach someone. Maybe one story, one success, one lesson will give you the courage to persevere and push through whatever obstacle or mental barrier that is holding you back from living the life of your dreams. Whether it's financial, social, spiritual, or emotional wealth you seek, the life you want for yourself is well within reach!

The year was 1973 and I vaguely remember being in Shafer Stadium, which is now Gillette Stadium, home of the New England Patriots. I was four and my mom, older brother and I were watching my dad play semi-pro football for the Rhode Island Raiders.

My dad was considered a freak of nature back in those days. He was a Tight End standing 6'2 weighing 225 pounds and ran a 4.4, 40-yard dash. Back then he had what most sports analysts today would say, "soft hands and game breaking speed." I remember games where he would have 4 and 5 touchdowns, racking up hundreds of yards. He damn near caught every ball thrown his way. One game he had 6 touchdowns! This caught the eye of the Miami Dolphins, Detroit Lions and Philadelphia Eagles. I never knew why the Patriots weren't on the list but that's neither here nor there at this point.

With those kinds of numbers, most would think he would have gone to the NFL. He had the speed, size, and skill, but my dad grew up poor. What does growing up poor have to do with his football career you might ask? Everything. As you continue to read, the connection will become clear.

My dad grew up on the West End of Providence, an urban section of Rhode Island. My grandmother was a single mother of three. She did the best she could to provide for her children but still, there was too much month at the end of the money. They grew up on welfare, food stamps, and no father figure in the home, an all too familiar story of urban America for people of color.

Although he was extremely close to his brother and sister, the "traditional" family unit was non-existent. To put it lightly, my dad had no love for his father. His father abandoned the family for a life in local bars with his brothers.

My dad's ethnicity is Cape Verdean, which is a mixture of African and Portuguese ancestry. The Cape Verde islands are located off the western coast of Africa near Dakar and Senegal. Depending on the island you're from, many Cape Verdeans are taught not to recognize their African ancestry.

With that being said, my dad's uncles never liked the idea of my dad's father marrying and having children with an African American woman. One day my dad's uncles gave my dad's father an ultimatum: Them or us, and his father chose his brothers. From that day forward, my dad loathed his father as most kids would in that situation.

Here's where I draw the connection as I begin to illustrate the lessons I've learned through the lens of my dad and my own personal experience. When I was working as the direct care staff at a group home, a question was raised during a professional development day. "When does abuse of a child begin?" What are your thoughts to that question? What answer would you have given?

Without going into all the answers, much of the staff shouted out particularly good responses. However, the one I heard from the clinical director struck a chord. He said abuse in a child begins during conception. Hmmm? Think about that for a minute.

Is it abuse when a woman is drinking alcohol during pregnancy? Is it abuse when a woman is doing drugs while pregnant? How about a woman who is in an emotionally, physically, or psychologically abusive relationship while pregnant? What about a woman in a state of depression while pregnant…is that considered abuse? Is it neglect or abuse when a woman doesn't have the means to adequately care for herself while pregnant? Remember, abuse doesn't have to be intentional. It can be totally circumstantial but nevertheless true. I want to make sure I'm being sensitive and nonjudgmental to anyone reading this.

I began to realize how much our environment shapes and conditions our thoughts. I believe the clinical director was right when he said abuse starts during conception. How a woman treats her mind and body or allows herself to be treated can have drastic effects on the child. The behaviors children exhibit that often continue into adulthood are learned behaviors. We learn to be good people or bad. We learn to say thank you, please, hold doors, not swear in public, respect our elder's, etcetera.

How many of these issues were present when my grandmother was pregnant with my dad and how many continued after birth? How did my dad become the dad and husband he is today when the stat sheets in these stories too often end in death, drugs, or prison? How? It's all about a survivor's mindset and a burning desire to never repeat the past. I believe when your WHY is so strong, you can accomplish anything.

I'm wondering if now you're starting to connect the dots. Notice how I call my dad, "dad" and his father, "father?" Let us not confuse being a dad with fathering children. There is a huge difference, and worth a sentence or two. I will never confuse or give credit to any man who "fathers" children and doesn't embrace being a dad! Any man can father a child, but a real man embraces every aspect of being in his child's life, physically, emotionally, socially, spiritually, and financially.

As I write this, looking back I realize that so many issues were present in my dad's life at a young age that made him who he is today. The issues that were present in his past were a constant reminder of what not to do. They had a profound effect on how he parented my brother and I. The decisions and sacrifices he made for his family came from a culmination of unbearable conditions no young child should have to endure.

My dad left high school after his junior year. I refuse to use the phrase "drop out" because that phrase can have a very negative connotation. From the outside looking in, the phrase can symbolize trouble, bothersome, unintelligent, disinterest, and in describing my dad, that was the furthest from the truth. (As a side note, I would encourage you to rethink using that phrase, as it does not apply to all who have left school).

My dad had to get a job so he could help the family with the finer things in life like, a place to live, food, heat, electricity, and hot water. If what I'm saying makes sense, he didn't drop out. He chose family responsibilities over school. This was a pivotal time in my dad's life. It was shaping his mindset and approach to life and his future.

In my life I've met so many people who have a similar story of what I call Dreams Deferred. If you're reading this and my dad's story touches home, you know the exact event, day, time, and year you had to grow up. Unfortunately, your circumstances didn't allow you to remain a child. You were thrust into adulthood long before your time and had to defer your childhood dreams. My heart goes out to you. Know you can push through and I hope this book helps.

I never really knew why my dad didn't make it to the NFL until later in life. My mom told me the coaches all but begged him to get to the camps. When it came time to make the decision to go to camp, the survivor mindset of a 17-year-old boy kicked in.

In order to make the team, he would have to get himself to the camps. He would have to pay for lodging, food, and transportation. All he could think about was the incurred cost it would take to go to the camps, and from what my dad told me, we simply didn't have it. He was married and had my mom, older brother, and I to care for. He couldn't fathom the thought of spending the money for "his" shot. It seemed selfish and reminded him of his father. He was committed to his family and made a decision that he would never be like his father. His children would never know what it meant to not have their dad in their lives. His wife would never feel the burden of wondering what bar he was in, would he get home safely, or come home at all. He would not leave his family, so again, Dreams Deferred.

How many people do you know who have an all too familiar story? Maybe it's you, the reader. I'm here to tell you there's hope. My goal in writing this is to inspire you to push through.

As the events of my dad's childhood unfolded and shaped his life, he has been my greatest inspiration. Not a day goes by where he doesn't think about what life could have been like had he found a way to get to those camps. Knowing my dad the way I do, he would have been an amazing NFL Tight End and would have never missed a beat as a dad!

Through his pain and struggle, he showed us strength. He ingrained in us a desire to build what you love. He taught us never to settle, and to always follow your dreams no matter what. He taught us the importance of always putting family first. He taught us to always love and respect your mother. Rachel C. Santos, you are the most amazing mother a son could ever ask for. This book is dedicated to my dad, Charles E. Santos Sr., a true definition of a dad, a hero, and an all-around great man!

CHAPTER 1

ROBBING THE CRATE

I remember it like it was yesterday. I was at my cousin Deidre Perry's wedding reception. It was being held in Wiggins Village on the south side of Providence, Rhode Island at a little banquet facility called The Hole in The Wall. All the family on my mother's side was there, and as always, we were laughing and reminiscing about past cookouts and family trips to Atlantic City. Suddenly, in came this medium height, darker-skinned young brother who was setting up the music. He couldn't have been more than 16-17 years old.

The year was 1979-1980 so I had to be 10 or 11 years of age. At that time, I had no idea what it was to be a DJ as I had never seen one. I had no idea what being a DJ entailed or the kind of equipment it took. When he was done setting up, he started playing music and it was a continuous flow that lasted the entire evening. No stoppages or breaks, ever! I looked over at him with a puzzled look because prior to this moment, all I knew was to play music one record at a time on my parents record player. I had no idea what he was doing but it was dope (that's hip-hop slang for "amazing")! I was very fond of music. Growing up my parents played it all throughout the house, especially on Saturday mornings when it was time to clean. If you grew up in my generation you know exactly what I am talking about. Things always seemed to get done faster with music. Chores on Saturday mornings were a lot more tolerable when mom and dad were blasting groups like the Delfonics, Stylistics, Manhattans, The O'Jays, and my dad's favorite, Gladys Knight and the Pips.

As I think back, after seeing and hearing the DJ play, I don't believe I gave any attention to anyone else in the family for the rest of the reception. I was fixated on this young man who was doing something I had never seen or heard before. How was he seamlessly moving from one song to the next? Enough time had passed, and I couldn't resist. I walked up to him and introduced myself. His name was Buck Collins and to the rest of the world he goes by DJ Buck. That chance meeting would forever change my life. He proceeded to answer every question I had about his equipment and the functionality. I was hooked! Looking back on my career, I owe so much to DJ Buck who continues to be a friend and confidant.

There's no DJ Finesse without DJ Buck. Here in Rhode Island he's considered a local legend but his presence in the music industry is much bigger – it's global. We are now older and he's since moved out of state, but when we bump into each other there's always mutual love, respect, admiration, and appreciation. I've learned that people don't have to be in your life daily to have an impact. Their impact can be as subtle as a chance meeting. When you come across people like DJ Buck, make sure you take a moment to thank them in whatever way you see fit. For me, it's only fitting I do it here.

The very next day I woke up early and moved the family record player into my room. I know what you may be asking yourself: Record player? Yes. If you have no idea what one is, or looks like, you were probably born after the year 2000. If that's the case, just Google record player and you can see what I am talking about. Ours was a one piece that had three sections. It had a record player on top, radio in the middle and cassette player on the bottom.

I started organizing my room to clear space for crates of records. I didn't bother to ask my parents; I just took what we had and what I knew to be the music I loved to hear. I grabbed every cassette tape my dad owned and began recording over his music. Boy was he pissed! He would get classic music from a friend of his who lived in Boston.

It was music we didn't hear in Rhode Island and he

noticed his collection dwindling. He would continually yell, "Who's taking my tapes?" Of course, it was me, but no way was I admitting to it. Till this day I still feel he knew it was me.

I began spending hours upon hours literally scratching every record we had until most sounded horrible to play. I must have worn out the grooves in so many records that when the needle glided over certain sections of the record, it had a distinct muffled sound.

Looking back at it now it's kind of funny seeing the look on my parents faces when they played them. I would cringe right before the part in the record played that I had scratched over and over. My parents would throw their hands in the air with a puzzled look and immediately look my way. I would just smile and shrug my shoulders.

Years passed and it was now 1984. I began investing in my new love. I had a job as a Dietary Aid in a local nursing home and used the money I made to buy necessary equipment. I remember DJ Buck had two Technique 1200 turntables, a mixer, and a lot of 12-inch records. Now, for clarity: 12-inch records were records that usually had only one song on them. They were singles from an album to be released at a later date. I would take the city bus with my best friend John Baptista to downtown Providence every Saturday to buy records at Rainbow Records.

John came to Rhode Island from New Jersey when he

was in the 9th grade. We met that year in Martin Jr. High in East Providence. He was the new kid in school, and I saw he had a dope way of dressing. I made it my business to get to know him and make him feel welcomed. I quickly found out that he loved music as much as I did. His personality and style for clothes were equally as flashy so we immediately became best friends. He lived on one side of a busy street and we lived on the other. We hung out every day! We did everything teens did in those days but for the purpose of this chapter what's important to know is he was there for the start of my music career. Every Saturday I would take some of the money I earned from working at the local nursing home and buy records. John and I would call one another on the phone and coordinate the time to leave our houses so that we would arrive at the bus stop at the same time.

Back then you could buy 12-inch single records for $1.99 and some for 99 cents. At that time Hip Hop had not gone mainstream but there were so many incredible artists like Run DMC, Whodini, LL Cool J, The Fat Boys, UTFO, Kurtis Blow, Jazzy Jeff & The Fresh Prince, and this list continues. Oftentimes John and I would buy the same record.

I knew DJ's had an uncanny way of extending a particular section of a song and in order to do that I needed two of the same records. I am not sure if he truly knows or understands how much of an instrumental role, he played in helping to establish the foundation of my career. I don't think I ever told him, so I wanted to make sure it was written in this book.

I started recording everything I did so I could listen back and attempt to get better. I started spinning all the local high school house parties. I spent hours upon hours trying to hone my skills, but the problem was I had no one to compare myself to. I had no teacher, so it was complete trial and error. In East Providence, no one was doing what I was doing. Remember this was the mid to late 80's and there was no Internet, no YouTube.

I remember listening to Jazzy Jeff & The Fresh Prince trying to figure out how to scratch. Teaching moment: Scratching happens when you move the record back and forth over and over on a specific section of the song. Different sounds happen depending on the speed and movement of your hands combined with the movement of the mixers crossfader. I was fascinated by what I was hearing and was determined to figure it out.

I remember the feeling I felt when I finally figured out how to Transform Scratch. I was in my basement and I remember continuously listening to "The Magnificent" by Dj. Jazzy Jeff & The Fresh Prince. It was one of the songs off their first album called "Rock The House". I remember sitting for hours, playing that record over and over, mesmerized, trying to figure out what Jazzy Jeff was doing to create this scratch he called "Transforming". To help you better understand; if you've ever watched one of the "Transformers" movies, there is a sound each Transformer makes when they "transform" from one form to another. Jazzy Jeff was able to manipulate the record and make that sound. Having no visual, I just kept moving the record back and forth with one hand while playing with the crossfader of the mixer with the other.

Now, for those of you who are unfamiliar, the mixer is a piece of equipment DJs use to toggle back and forth from one turntable to the next. Depending on how you manipulate the mixer and the record, you can create some amazing sounds. On this particular day I remember being tireless in my effort to figure out how to transform. Then, all of a sudden, bam! For a split second I heard the sound!

You would have thought I hit the lottery! I was jumping up and down pumping my fist in the air and I immediately called John. When he answered I yelled at him to get to my house as soon as possible! John was there within minutes. I met him at the door and damn near pushed him down the stairs to the basement. I got behind the turntables and showed him what I had discovered. To this day John is the only one with the first DJ Finesse mix cassette. He proudly brandishes the fact that he still has it in his possession.

The year is 1988 and I am a sophomore at the University of Rhode Island. I am torn because I am in love with two women. One is Hip Hop, and the other is basketball. I split my time equally between the two. I remember being one of a few students on campus that had DJ equipment in his room. I also remember being one of the students invited to try out for the basketball team. The basketball story I will save for another chapter.

I remember placing a speaker in the window and playing music so loud that students passing under my dorm window could hear. I remember having close to 25 people in our dorm room at one time. It was truly party central. It's absolutely the reason why my grades were so poor. I did just enough to stay on campus. My grades and education were the least of my focus. I'd have to say at that time in my life, music took precedence.

I purposely chose to leave the story of DJ Finesse for another book that may be written one day. Know that I have a music career that has lasted 35 years. I am not sure what year you purchased your copy of, "From Personal to Purpose", but as of 2020 I am still actively spinning in my 50s.

I have traveled all over the continental US and abroad. I have been on television, radio, and the big screen. I was blessed to have a musical ear and a work ethic that opened the door to become a celebrity DJ for one of the most prestigious and successful record labels in the history of Hip Hop. I have met tons of celebrities and have been in, and around the celebrity circuit. I have walked red carpets. I have done events for the NBA as well as the NFL. Traveling the world gave me a chance to meet so many people. Every encounter was a teachable moment. I have learned a great deal from people, and about people. The lessons I have learned along the way are shared throughout this book.

I believe my story will be a lot of things to a lot of people. This book is my attempt to reach and inspire as many people as possible through my life experiences. What this book is not is the full story of DJ Finesse. That may be a good read one day.

Let me apologize now to you, the reader who thought this was a book solely about the life of a DJ. The lessons I've learned that I share with you have truly inspired me to write this book. I needed to give you the back-story to help you understand my passion and purpose. The only way we connect the dots is by looking back and attempting to understand what got us to this point in our lives.

As I reminisce about this period in my life, I was learning lessons I had no idea I was learning. As you read this book, each chapter is a key element needed in order to be successful. Some may seem so simple but if you miss them, you may never find your true calling in life and opportunities may continue to pass you by.

Opportunities are never wasted...
they simply go to the next person!

The chapters are not in chronological order so feel free to skip around if one title seems more interesting than the other. Please do yourself the favor and read them all. I believe something in these chapters is for everyone. Something I say, a story I tell, a quote I reference from another amazing author, just may provide your breakthrough. I strongly encourage you to read, take notes and even highlight so you can come back to it later.

At the end of each chapter I want you to reflect on the information you just read. Sit with it for a moment and think how this relates to you. I need you to be totally honest with yourself. If my stories and lessons are to be of any use to you, I am asking you to be vulnerable.

What lessons did you learn and how do my stories resonate with you? I want you to start connecting your dots. I want you to look back at the decisions you made that got you to this point in your life and jot them down in the space I have provided.

Maybe it was a specific incident or decision you made in a particular time period that moved you forward or set you back. Was it a teachable moment and did you learn from it? This is your personal space, your journal, your thoughts, your memories, your journey. Use the time and space wisely and turn your Personal into Purpose!

FROM
PERSONAL
TO
PURPOSE

CHAPTER 2

YOU ONLY KNOW WHAT YOU KNOW

What we focus on expands.
If you focus on obstacles,
you will get more problems.
If you focus on possibilities, you
will create more opportunities.

I realize now that the lessons I learned from my immediate family and environment had almost everything to do with my success and failures. It's amazing what can happen when you commit to personal development.

Learning about yourself and a desire to improve can become as habitual as smoking cigarettes. My mentor Martin Ruof would always tell me, "You need to know more than you know." When he first made that statement, it wasn't as clear today as it was when I first heard it. I had to stop and think a bit because I knew Martin to be a thinker.

Every time I sit with him I am amazed at the information and knowledge he possesses. He is an extremely gifted and talented speaker. His advice is immeasurable. He tells me if I am to continue growing as a person, I will need to position myself around people who outthink me and try to outthink them. This continues to serve me to this day, and I believe it will serve you if you put this into practice.

Life is a culmination of teachable moments, all of which are good and bad, but nevertheless, extremely valuable for our personal development. All of us come into situations and relationships with prior knowledge. Things we learn from our parents, family, friends, community, and environment creates our own personal thinking pattern we use to make decisions.

How we act and react to situations varies from person to person. No two thinking patterns are the same as we all encounter different people, have different families, come from diverse backgrounds, communities, and cultures. Our thought process may be similar, but everyone's thinking pattern is unique. I have realized that even in our uniqueness, we need to continually upgrade our thinking.

Have you ever known someone who continues to make the same mistakes over and over? We all have a friend, family member or colleague that seems to be in the thick of it all the time. It's almost as if they invite chaos. Our natural response for these people is that he or she brought it upon himself or herself. In most cases I would say you are correct, and you have every right to agree or disagree.

The stance you take or the argument you make that they indeed bring things on themselves, you make based on your prior knowledge. The point I am trying to make is what we focus on expands. Our thoughts become actions, both positive and negative. Positive thinking almost always leads to positive actions and outcomes as negative thinking almost always leads to negative actions and outcomes.

Most of us have heard the phrase, "think outside the box." Your thinking pattern is your box. Thinking errors occur when we refuse to personally develop and go beyond what we know inside our box. As long as we continue to think with our surface level pattern, we fail to grow, we fail to learn.

Thinking errors are as inevitable as the tide coming in. The goal is to continually develop and modify the patterns so that we can reduce the amount of friction in our lives. We must be willing to go beyond what we know and explore deeper meaning and perspectives.

Marc Accetta is one of the most sought-after trainers in Network Marketing. He is a master in personal development, public and motivational speaking. He has an innate ability to motivate people to be the best version of themselves. He's spent over 30 years in MLM and personal development. I sat in one of his seminars and he made a statement that had such a profound effect on how I viewed life. He said, "People only know what they know, and they don't know what they don't know." If what he was saying were true, most will never upgrade their thinking pattern on their own. I immediately began thinking about my own pattern. I only began to upgrade my pattern because I had mentors who had an interest in my success and saw areas I would need to develop and improve if I wanted to attain the level of success I desired.

Maybe you have mentors who are invested in your success as are mine. If not, maybe this chapter can be the bridge between where you are, and where you desire to be in life. My goal is to help you understand what it means to only know what you know.

What I have noticed is that too many people focus on everything and everyone else. This is fine if you're following the right people, the ones who have what you want. If not, it's a thinking error and you may want to upgrade your circle of influence. Find people who have what you want, do what they do so you can have what they have. That is exactly what successful people do. My goal is to become a motivational speaker, so I constantly listen to people like Eric Thomas, Les Brown, Tony Robbins, and Jim Rohn.

The approach you take is your own and know it is not written in stone that you will achieve the exact same level of success of the people you are studying. What I will hang my hat on is who you follow may be just as important as who you desire to become so the results you desire begin with you.

The late great Jim Rohn, one of the most famous of all network marketers, famous for inspiring millions to reach greatness states,

"Don't wish it was easier, you should wish you were better!"

Don't wish for less problems, wish for more skills. Lastly, don't wish for less challenges, wish for more wisdom." Realize that for things to change, you have to change. If you are to be successful, you must upgrade your current knowledge no matter the industry.

Average people do average things. When we say someone is above average it's because he or she has done more or is willing to do more than the average person is willing to do. Very few are willing to pay the price to become successful. I remember Hall of Fame NFL wide receiver Jerry Rice saying...

"Today I will do what others won't, so tomorrow I will have what others can't!"

It's such a profound statement that goes to the heart of what we're talking about in this chapter. Knowing you have to do more than what most are willing to do is an example of having to know more than you know. It's upgrading your thinking pattern.

Getting comfortable being uncomfortable is where growth happens.

I am here to tell you, you're not alone. I was doing a talk in front of a group of people one evening about life and opportunity. My friend Angel was in the crowd and I wanted to make a point to my audience, most of whom were not satisfied with where they wanted to be in life. They all wanted more, but again, there needed to be an upgrade to their thinking patterns. They only knew what they knew.

To illustrate my point, and not to embarrass anyone, I asked my friend Angel a question. I chose Angel because he heard this talk before and knew exactly the point I was trying to make. In front of the room I asked Angel a very simple question. I asked him, "how much is two plus two?" Angel replied, "four." I repeated the question again, and again Angel replied, "four."

I proceeded to ask him again in a different tone as if to imply he may be wrong. Again, Angel replied, "four."

I asked him if he was sure and he replied, "yes." I asked him if he was absolutely positive that two plus two equals four, and again, but hesitantly, he replied, "Yes, I am sure it's four." The crowd laughed because they thought it was a trick question. After all, a third grader knows two plus two equals four.

I then said to Angel, "That's interesting. You've been telling me all along you wanted to get to five, but you keep adding two plus two knowing it's four. As a matter of fact, you said you were absolutely positive that two plus two is four." I then proceeded to ask Angel, "Try adding two plus three?" Angel responded, "five." My eyebrows raised and I gave Angel and my audience a look of surprise and amazement.

After a silent pause I said to the audience, "Wow! A slight change, a slight upgrade in thinking, a small shift in thinking outside of your box got you EXACTLY where you wanted to be!" You only know what you know, and you don't know what you don't know, but, when you know, there's still more you have to know. As soon as you understand this concept, the modification to your thinking pattern begins.

The mind is like an iPhone operating system: It constantly has to be updated if it is to work properly.

Failure to grasp this concept is the true definition of insanity, because two plus two will never equal five.

One afternoon I was sitting with a good friend of mine, Maximo. Max as we call him is incredibly successful. He made the bulk of his money in graphics and marketing straight out of college. He is the guy everyone goes to when you need help expanding on a big idea. He sees things most don't. He sees the good in everything and in everyone. He has an uncanny ability to get the best out of people and ideas to help them see what they can become.

What's most incredible about Max, is that he does it out of the kindness of his heart. He is the guy everyone wants to follow, and everyone wants to pay but he rarely takes a dime. Max is one of my most influential mentors, so when he talks, I make sure to listen.

As we sat in a coffee shop, we were talking about success and he made a statement I felt was fitting for this chapter. He told me there are no such things as failures, only lessons. I had never thought about it that way. If that statement is true then the only people who utterly fail are those who quit, give up or fail to learn from their mistakes.

I want you to begin looking at all your experiences as learning experiences. Some will be good and some not so good, but all learning. When I look at people and attempt to understand why some are immensely successful and others are not, I am amazed at the pressure people put on themselves to succeed. They fall in love with success and not the process.

Most compare themselves to others and at that very moment, the dream dies.

> *Comparison is the*
> *thief of all dreams.*
> *When you compare yourself*
> *to others, you are*
> *abandoning your race.*

You begin running someone else's race. We begin looking at what we don't have instead of creating what we want. Back in our day we called this trying to live like the "Jones." Look at the Jones' new home, then suddenly, "We should get a similar home." Wow, look at the Jones' new car! All of a sudden, "We need a car like that." Wow, look at Mr. Jones' new wardrobe! All of a sudden we find ourselves at the mall on a shopping spree. I see it all the time. Each one of us was put on this earth to run our own race. Although the destination may be the same, no two people run the identical race.

Have you ever watched track and field? If you ever get a chance to watch a track and field event, take a minute to watch the 1600-meter race. If you watch that event, you will notice each runner, no matter his or her lane assignment, has the same 1600 meters to run. Every time I've watched this event, there are always a few runners who get out of the blocks fast. Every time I watch, I say to myself, "There's no way he or she can keep up that pace," and every time I am right. They never win.

Conversely, look at the best long-distance runners. They are the runners who understand pace and process. They understand although everyone has the same goal or destination, no two runners are the same. You will always hear their coaches telling them to run their race; pace YOURSELF. The race is theirs to run just like life.

Success in life is a long-distance race, not a sprint.

In order to be successful, you have to commit to controlled consistent output over the length of your life's race. Remember, we only know what we know so this mindset takes practice and training in order to develop.

I mentioned in the beginning of this book there is a direct connection between success and a person's life experiences. I also mentioned in this chapter that we only know what we know. My parents taught my brother and I love. They showed us every day what love looked like, sounded like, and what love felt like.

There wasn't a day that went by where my parents didn't tell us they loved us. They made sure we knew the words were never empty and followed them up with daily physical gestures of affection. They hugged us, they laughed with us, they cried with us, but most importantly, they were genuinely interested in what we were interested in.

Having a support system of people who want to see you win and push you to be great is an amazing feeling. Every child wants to feel important. Every child wants to know mom and dad care. Every child wants and deserves affection. Every child wants to feel like his/her dreams are important and encouraged. Unfortunately, so many will never know the feeling.

As amazing as our home life was, there were some hard lessons I had to learn. Looking back now I am amazed at how I wasn't able to see the forest through the trees. What I realize now is, when you're growing up, life does not always reveal its secrets to us.

Life is tricky. It tests us to see how bad we want something and what we're willing to go through to achieve it. Some have an easier path to success because success principles were taught in the home. We don't all start from the same place but we all, at one time or another, get an opportunity to run our own race as I mentioned earlier. How you perform in life's race has a lot to do with the lessons we pick up along the way.

I was a good basketball player in high school, but I was a late bloomer. I was 5'5" as a senior but luckily I grew seven inches in my first three years of college. I attended the University of Rhode Island straight out of high school. As I tell this story, towards the end, the lesson will become clear.

I didn't know what it took to play Division 1 basketball. I only knew what I knew. Although my dad and brother were very good, neither of them played division 1 basketball. My brother earned a division two scholarship to Bryant College, now Bryant University. He was really good, and I believe he could have played at a division 1 school.

What I remember most growing up was playing basketball almost every day! If you wanted to find me, you went to Silver Spring Elementary School and checked the basketball court. Unlike today's athletes, we didn't have AAU, we didn't have trainers, and we damn sure didn't have the Internet and YouTube.

If you wanted to know who was really good, you had to seek them out, it was all word of mouth. The better I became the more names were thrown at me of players others thought were better or who could pose a challenge. I remember as early as 12, specifically hearing the names Matt Gonsalves, and Tony Gomes. Matt was from East Providence like me and he literally was the one player that motivated me to play every day. Tony, I didn't worry about too much because he moved to California, but you can believe when he came back to Rhode Island to visit, everyone let me know.

We had no way to see other players across the country. There was no way to see how good they were. We didn't have the countless basketball camps today's basketball players have. The only camp I remember hearing about was 5-Star and we couldn't afford to go so we never asked. I don't believe my parents knew about 5-Star, so it was never an issue. You can't miss something you've never had, so what we knew was playing at the parks and playgrounds.

In my first three years of college I played more basketball than ever. The talent of players not playing for the team was better than my high school talent. I played for hours every day and it showed when grades came out. I did just enough to stay in school.

By my junior year I was now 6'0" and man I was good. I was really good! I was fast, could handle the ball, shoot, and defend. I remember playing with the basketball team and did more than hold my own. My skill became so noticeable, people I played pickup with, as well as players from the team were telling me I should attempt to walk on.

I remember one day in my dorm room I was cutting Kenny Green's hair. Everyone on campus cut hair back in those days to earn some spending money. Kenny stood about 6'9". He was an All-American and he was the captain of the men's basketball team. To this day I swear he gave me the biggest compliment that I wish I had never heard!

I remember him telling me the head coach, who at the time was Al Skinner, was looking for a few dummy players. Dummy players were those players whose role would be simplified to practice players. They most likely would only be useful in practices and possibly see the court in the end of game, or blowout situations. He then proceeded to tell me, "The way you play, you could actually get some playing time".

Here is the lesson. I didn't know what it took to play division one. I only knew what I knew. I had no one to tell me what I was supposed to do and why. When I heard that statement, what I heard was, you are good enough already.

I met with coach Al Skinner and he told me I needed to go to pre-season conditioning. Why do that I thought? I was more than handling my own in team pickup games. I figured I would just go to the gym more and work on skill development and that's exactly what I did. I played for hours working on my skill but that was it.

I attended the first pre-season conditioning session at 6am and never went again. My earliest class was at 10am. I remember thinking why get up that early if I was already having success. Remember, Kenny Green, the All- American just told me I was going to get actual minutes! I know, I know! I know exactly what any basketball player reading this, or, any scholarship athlete reading this is thinking. Let me spare you the words and say it for you, "You fool!" This is exactly the lesson I want you to understand in this chapter.

I really want you to grasp this lesson! We only know what we know. It wasn't ego that kept me from going to pre-season workouts. It wasn't me thinking I was better than everyone else. I was confident but ignorant to what it took to play at that level.

Looking back at that moment in time, connecting the dots, I obviously had no clue. In my mind this was Silver Spring all over again. This was the playground. Just go out there and play. Play more and you will be fine. When the day came for tryouts I did exceedingly well. Unfortunately, after the first 60 minutes it was all downhill. It all came crashing down! Fatigue started kicking in. My thighs started to swell and cramp. I had no wind. I started to feel nausea. They ran me into the ground and did it with no basketballs.

Other ball players attempting to walk on were killing me! These were players who couldn't hold my jock. Players I would dominate in pickup games. But this was no pick-up game. This was the real deal and they took it seriously. They went to every pre-season conditioning session. No way we're they more talented. They were better prepared. Hard work and dedication will beat talent every time and Kudos to every player that walked on that year.

I remember at the end of a three-hour tryout, Al Skinner had all the players attempting to walk on play 3-on-3 full court. I thought to myself, this is it, I must dig deep, and I did. I dominated in my last attempt to prove I was better than the rest. Unfortunately, the story does not go where I say I did so well in that 3-on-3 that I made the team. It's just the opposite. My friend Marc Fears was the team statistician at the time. May God rest his soul as he passed away far too early.

I remember at the end of the tryout Marco as we called him, pulled me aside and asked me if I wanted to know why I didn't make the team? He told me all the coaches were talking and when it came time for my evaluation, they asked about Santos. As I remember Marco telling me, Al Skinner said, "He's good, he's really good, but not that good where he does not have to show up to pre-season conditioning."

What a lesson! Although I needed more size, I lacked commitment necessary to get bigger and stronger. Although I had the speed, I needed to learn the importance of sacrifice. Although I had the skill set, I lacked knowledge. My not making the team wasn't for a lack of talent. I didn't make the team because I lacked character. Who I was at that time was not who they were looking for.

I believe people don't plan
to fail, they fail to plan...
and I failed miserably.

I am often asked if I could have played division 1 basketball and in my earlier years I would answer with an astounding, "hell yes!" Looking back, that was me trying to justify the result in my head to my heart.

It's taken some time to get to a point where I now say, "absolutely not." Did I have the skill, I believe so, but actually playing, I didn't have what it takes. I didn't plan. I didn't prepare. I didn't upgrade my knowledge and put myself in the best position to be successful. I only knew what I knew which was to go to the gym and play.

As I write this book, I can't help but reference the amazing author Marshall Goldsmith who wrote a book titled "What Got You Here, Won't Get You There". Man, that couldn't be truer. What I did to get myself into that division one tryout was not nearly enough for me to make the team. I am here to tell you that just knowing isn't enough!

If you are going to be successful, you are going to have to sacrifice. You are going to have to upgrade your knowledge. You are going to have to get out of your comfort zone.

Being comfortable only leads to mediocrity.

I believe every person can be successful beyond his or her wildest dreams. The problem is most will not do what it takes to reach their goals. Most will ignore instruction and advice from someone who has achieved success in the very field they are interested in.

Most, like myself in that tryout will question the process and continue to do things his or her way. We start making excuses and exceptions. We dumb down the goal believing it's still the goal. In doing so we've created a different goal we believe is more attainable because we didn't have the fortitude, desire, dedication, or commitment to see the initial goal through. We weren't willing to sacrifice who we are for who we want to become.

> *We convince ourselves that our way is better when it's actually the excuse we give ourselves, so we don't have to put in the work.*

The question we must ask ourselves is, "If what you're doing now could give you the results you wanted, wouldn't you already have them?" Most choose not to stand in the mirror and ask the person they see the tough questions.

Charles Barkley, one of the NBA's 50 greatest players made a statement once during an interview that has stuck with me and I will reference it here. He said, "Potential means you ain't shit right now!" He continued to say, "Anything in life worth having is not going to be easy to obtain." I couldn't agree more. If success in anything were easy, everyone would have it. And at that point, the accomplishment would no longer be special.

When asked what he meant by his statements, he proceeded to tell the story of a conversation he had with his head basketball coach Sonny Smith his freshman year at Auburn. Charles said one day coach Smith came to him after practice and told him he thought he had the "potential" of being one of the best power forwards ever to play in the NBA. He said his coach stressed the word "potential" because at that time, Smith felt Charles was lazy. He felt Charles wasn't living up to his "potential" by putting in the work and sacrifice necessary to be great.

He told Charles he was lazy and out of shape. Charles could have started making excuses and exceptions. Instead, he took it personally. He took personal inventory of himself and the amazing opportunity he had in front of him. He trusted the person who had been successful and committed to the process of becoming great. To make a long story short, not only did he become a first team collegiate All-American; he had an amazing NBA career, became an Olympic champion as a part of the "Dream Team," and was named one of the NBA's 50 greatest players.

I say all this to say, we must know more than we know. Not only do we have to elevate our knowledge in our perspective field of interest, but to achieve success you are going to have to personally develop. Change is difficult. If you ask any successful person, the majority will tell you success came only when they decided to upgrade their knowledge and commit to knowing more than they know.

TAKEAWAYS

Does it make sense that you have to upgrade your knowledge if you are to be successful in anything? To no fault of my own, can you see how only knowing what I knew wasn't enough? As you can see there are specific sentences and thoughts bolded and italicized for you to reference when needed. These thoughts, ideas and concepts continue to serve me. How will this chapter serve you? What was your takeaway? Were there any "Ah Ha" moments for you? Use this space to jot the lessons you learned from this chapter below.

CHAPTER 3

THE SURFER MINDSET

Let me start this chapter by saying I have never surfed. I have never been on a surfboard and I make no claims about the sport. One day I was sitting at my desk and I was thinking to myself, why are some people successful while others are not? It came to me that almost every person who has reached a high level of success was, or is, a forward-thinker. For some strange reason I thought about surfers and the sport of surfing. I started looking up images of surfers on the Internet and three images helped me create this chapter.

The first image that immediately caught my attention depicted a slew of surfers sitting on their boards in the ocean peering around. Not only did it look as though they were looking for the right wave, they were also looking at each other.

The thought occurred to me that very few people are

true leaders, and most are followers. The second image that caught my eye was an image of a surfer lying on his board paddling ferociously. In that picture he was by himself. There were no signs of any surfers, or any wave behind him. This observation is extremely important in making my point, which I will do shortly. Lastly, and surely not the least of importance was an image of that lone surfer standing upright riding a huge wave. What's also extremely important to note is that the image captured a host of surfers positioned near the top just behind the crest of the wave, and more sitting on their boards even further behind.

I began thinking about the direct correlation between a surfer's mindset and that of successful people. What kind of forward thinking goes into being a great surfer? On the surface, like myself, most see the courage, bravery, athleticism, balance, stance, skill, technique, and of course the surfboard itself. I can honestly say looking back at my impression of surfing, that's all I noticed when I was younger. Now, I see something totally different.

What is it that makes one surfer better than the others? One might say practice, commitment, drive, or ambition, all true I might add. All those attributes have to exist in order to perfect one's craft but here is where I draw the distinction between those surfers who are good versus those who become great; those who are successful and those who fail to achieve success. It begins with this statement:

I have never seen a surfer win a competition without catching a wave. Show me a surfer who fails to catch a wave and I will show you a surfer in the middle of the ocean.

As I began thinking about this concept I was blown away. Some of the greatest surfers, like most successful people, are the ones who see the waves before they form. This is true of any successful person. Successful people, like surfers, are the ones who see the "wave" of opportunity others don't see. Successful people take calculated risk. They understand...

without risk there can be no reward,

so they confidently stand up on the board. Successful people don't follow the crowd, and most don't do what they do for the applause. They understand that recognition is a reward for maximum effort, commitment, sacrifice and hard work. They aren't concerned with "the other guy" unless the other guy has a blueprint worth following.

They don't sit around looking left or right. They see an opportunity most don't, and they paddle. I am here to tell you in order to be successful you're going to have to paddle forward to position yourself to catch the wave of opportunity. So many people fail because they miss opportunities.

> *What people don't realize is opportunities aren't missed... they just go to the next person who is ready, and willing to act.*

So, why do so many miss the wave of opportunity? After talking to hundreds of people I realized so many fail to see the big picture, surround themselves with the wrong people, are afraid of change, and/or simply don't want to put in the hard work. They believe a real opportunity is supposed to present itself full-blown, operational, and knock on their front door. That is the farthest from the truth.

Opportunities come and go like waves, like the tide in the ocean. So why is it that some succeed, and others don't? I must admit it: Even I was one of those people who felt like others were just pure lucky. They seemed to always be in the right place at the right time. They were always working on something and for the life of me I couldn't figure out how.

Now, I am here to tell you if you ask any successful person, he or she will tell you their success had little to do with luck and everything to do with preparation and action. My mentor Max always says, "you can be in the right place at the right time, but if you aren't prepared to take action, it's as if you weren't even there!" For you the reader, I strongly urge you to read and reread this book and others like it. Personally develop yourself so you can recognize the wave of opportunity, take action, start paddling and put yourself in position to win.

I was listening to an audio of Jim Rohn one day while driving, and he said...

> *"We are the average of the five people you spend the most time with."*

Looking at my circle I realized this was true. I have some of the most amazing friends. Most of my friends I consider to be family. Most of us met in college and the relationships we forged on those campuses are as strong today as they were back then.

Ironically, when it came to understanding what I wanted to achieve professionally and personally, I had to adopt another circle. This by no means is a slight to any of my friends who are reading this. Forging new relationships in your industry is extremely vital to your success.

The relationships I have with the friends I consider family are amazing. Our conversations center around a genuine love for one another and our families. The fun we have when we get together and start reminiscing about the past always breaks out in knee slapping laughter. If you have this with your friends, you are blessed.

For me though, I wanted to create something special beyond the walls of our group. I have always had this burning desire to create something bigger than me, something bigger than all of us. I wanted to do something or be something the world could relate to. I wanted to live a life of purpose and inspire others to be the best version of themselves.

It dawned on me that in my circle, we weren't having those conversations. We weren't talking about future plans and combining resources and ideas to help each other grow personally and professionally and there is absolutely nothing wrong with that. Realize as you continue to grow and move towards your goals you will grow into different circles of people who share similar interests.

> *You must maintain balance.*
> *Growing into your professional*
> *circle, does not mean forget*
> *about your family circle.*

I remember when I left my 9 to 5 job to work on my own business in the travel industry, one of my closest friends mentioned to me that our circle of friends couldn't understand why I would choose to leave the security of a job.

At first, I was a bit jaded, but it was at that point I knew exactly what Jim Rohn was talking about. My friends are all amazing people, but they don't see what I see. The goals and dreams I have in my heart are mine to pursue. We all choose different paths and as close as you may be with your circle, it's not their job to join you simply because they are your friends.

We all have interests that others may see no value in. Your friends and family may not want what you want, but it does not mean they don't want to see you succeed.

One of my closest friends is Jose. He is extremely talented and is pursuing a career in acting. In just three short years he has gained a lot of attention and has been casted regularly. To do this, he's had to put himself in places and surround himself with people who can help him achieve his ultimate goal of getting on, and being seen in major movie productions.

Let me illustrate my point this way. If you have a snake as a pet, know it will never outgrow its cage. It will adapt to its environment. If you want the snake to grow, continue to upgrade the size of its cage. Humans are the same way. If you are to be successful, you are going to have to surround yourself with like-minded people. You are going to have to keep updating your social cage so you can grow and blossom into the person you were destined to become.

Find people who not only have what you want, but

who are also willing to help you achieve your goals. The unfortunate truth is you will have to sacrifice some time with your family and friends. They are your family and friends so make sure you sit them down and explain your goals and the vision you have for your future, most will understand.

So, why is there a huge disparity between those who are successful and those who are not, those who achieve the life of their dreams and others who settle for comfort? The problem most people have is they only see the finished product, the shiny object. They fall in love with the prize and not the process. They only see the wave when it's completely formed.

Most fail to see the sacrifice, commitment, and dedication to detail it takes to be successful. They conveniently browse over the chapter in life that talks about the blood, sweat, and tears it takes to get to the good life.

There can be no prize without pain.
Most fail to put themselves in
positions to win because they are
not willing to go through the pain.

I have a mentor who is immensely successful. I have been around him now for the past 5 years. If listening to him and following his lead were a college exam, I would be expelled for cheating! One day Martin and I were talking, and I asked him how he viewed others in his field, and he gave me two responses. He said, "Success leaves clues." He only paid attention to those who he considered to be more successful than he was.

He told me to surround myself with people who outthink me and try to outthink them. What he was saying was true growth and learning happens when we decide to change our circle of influence. Again, let me be clear: This is not about severing ties with your family and friends. It's about having the ability to separate personal from business and it's not always easy as I mentioned in the earlier paragraph.

So, how do the best separate themselves from the pack? They're fearless. Fear can stifle the best of talents.

I have a friend and mentor Mike Marich. He is an amazing public speaker. He travels all over the world talking to thousands about conquering fear. He states that to be successful, you have to...

Get comfortable being uncomfortable.

Getting uncomfortable for many means facing your fears. One of his best talks came in the form of a video he created from a graveyard. As he walked through the graveyard, he was pointing his camera at hundreds of headstones. As he walked past the headstones, he proceeded to say the graveyard is the richest place on earth.

When he made that statement, I wasn't sure the point he was trying to make. As I watched the video, all I could see were headstones and the thousands of people who had come and gone. I didn't make the connection between wealth and death. He continued by stating that the graveyard is the place where all the dreams, goals, ideas, and inventions people had died. He said one thing killed them all: FEAR! Fear killed all their dreams, goals, ideas, and thoughts for inventions. Fear of what people might say or think, fear that people won't understand you, fear that someone may not agree with you, fear if you can do it or not, or fearing if what you are working on will work or not.

How many of you are willing to cast fear aside to achieve success? How many of you will do what's necessary to put yourselves in the best position to win? You must see the opportunity before it forms, and you have to be ready. This is the surfer's mindset successful people have.

They don't wait, they take action. They aren't worried about being part of the crowd. They're not concerned with other surfers. Their minds are set on the goal. They look for waves where most wouldn't. They push fear aside and lead with courage and a will to win.

Winning for surfers is catching that wave they know every surfer wants to catch. Opportunities give successful people a rush just like waves do for surfers. They understand that like the ocean, success isn't a straight climb. Success is an ebb and flow motion like waves in the sea. There are ups and downs but for a successful person, there is no such thing as failure. It's all lessons. If you learn from your mistake it's a teachable moment.

Zig Ziglar states...

> *"If you are not willing to learn,*
> *no one can help you.*
> *If you are determined to learn,*
> *no one can stop you."*

So, time and time again they fall off their boards, never quitting because every time is a chance to learn.

Success is a process we all must learn to respect. During this process you will fail time and time again. Failure is a part of the process, quitting is not. In every failure there is a lesson if we are humble enough to admit we've made some mistakes, learn, and push through.

> *One thing I know for sure*
> *is quitters never win*
> *and winners never quit.*

When you fall off your surfing board, in a figurative sense - and you will fall off - get back on and paddle out again. Trust the process and trust the lessons each wave of life will teach you. In my life I have caught some big waves. I remember seeing waves of opportunity others couldn't see. You have a gift and your gift will continue to create opportunities. It's a success instinct you possess or that gut feeling very few can explain. Harness that power and let it continue to propel you forward. If you never quit, I can promise you there will be more waves to catch.

TAKEAWAYS

Look back on your life and try to identify a wave of opportunity you missed. Ask yourself what was it that kept you from acting on it? Since that moment of inaction, do you know of, or have you seen others flourishing in that opportunity you passed on? Embrace that feeling of loss. It can be a powerful tool and motivator if you're willing to learn from it. Opportunities are going to continue to come your way but if you don't act, you will be floating on your board in the middle of the ocean forever waiting. What lessons did you learn from this chapter? What are your takeaways?

_____
_____
_____
_____
_____
_____
_____
_____
_____
_____
_____
_____
_____
_____
_____
_____
_____
_____
_____
_____
_____
_____
_____

CHAPTER 4

THE KING

As you read this chapter the lesson will become clear as I tell you the story of the king. I want this chapter to be entertaining but I also want to make sure you don't miss the point. I believe the story of the king is a great way to illustrate another facet of success.

Once upon a time there was a rich king. Unlike most kings who rule their kingdom with tyranny, this king was very different. He came into power through hard work, determination, and a genuine love for his town's people. He provided goods and services to other kingdoms, and by doing so he created generational wealth. He had the finest gold, silver, diamonds, rubies, and emeralds. Although extremely wealthy, his goal was never to rule over his subjects.

He wanted to inspire, encourage, and add value to the

lives of all who lived in the kingdom. He embraced how he came into power, how he amassed his wealth, and was willing to teach anyone in the kingdom that wanted to learn. He was the kind of king who was always accessible and often seen among the people. He understood one of the most important laws of John C. Maxwell's, "21 Irrefutable Laws of Leadership":

> ### *People don't care how much you know until they know how much you care.*

As a side note, if leadership is your calling and you desire to become a better leader, I'd advise you to get this book.

This is a huge lesson I learned later in life. Some of us are only concerned with how much we know and the need to be right instead of how much we care and the need to be humble. If success is what you seek, know you will catch more bees with honey than vinegar.

There is no way I can continue this point without also referencing Dale Carnegie's, "How to Win Friends and Influence People." I read this book and it instantly changed my way of thinking. If you have not read this book, I strongly urge you to stop what you're doing and order it! The minute I finished reading it, I went back and read it again. Each time I read it I found new meaning. I immediately started calling my newfound insight "OPP."

You might remember a classic song called "OPP" recorded by a New Jersey Hip Hop group, Naughty by Nature. It's a song promoting cheating on your significant other. Putting it nicely and keeping this book rated PG, "OPP" stood for "Other People's Property."

As I continue to personally develop, OPP for me stands for "Other People's Perspective." Dale Carnegie's book had such a profound effect on how I viewed people. I finally started to understand that each person is uniquely different. Each person brings a unique perspective to every situation.

Looking back, I remember countless conversations where I had a need to be right. Time after time I totally dismissed the other person's perspective. What an idiot I was! If I knew I was right, boy were you in for it. I had no interest in your point of view. You know those people you can see thinking of an answer while you were trying to get your point across? I was that person, never paying attention to the other person speaking.

God help me if you ended your part of the conversation with a question. My clever response to get out of the jam would be, "Help me better understand your position," hoping you would restate the question. I had my position and I was dug in. I was going to make sure you knew I was right. Well, the joke was on me. If arguing a point of view was a sport, I would have been considered an All-Star. If persuading people to side with me because I valued their point of view was a sport, I would have been considered a bench player at best.

The king understood this concept and he, unlike early me, not only enjoyed OPP, he welcomed them. He knew with great power comes great responsibility. He had the power to be liked or feared.

He knew fear paralyzes most people and they fail to act on any level.

He wasn't interested in "yes men." He wanted a community of people free to act, explore ideas, and create lasting relationships. He knew if he treated everyone with respect and dignity he would be loved, and he was.

The king had a beautiful wife. They were happily married and together they had 7 daughters ranging from ages 5 to 18. Each of his daughters were as stunning as their mother, extremely talented and intelligent. Each year the king would hold a contest for all the young men in the kingdom.

Any young man 18 or older would have an opportunity to marry one of his daughters on her 18th birthday. The winner would not only be immensely wealthy, they would marry into the most beloved family in the land. On the same day of one of his daughters' 18th birthday, people from miles around would come to the kingdom to see if any young man were brave enough to accept the king's challenge.

Hundreds and hundreds of town's people would stand on the water's edge and peer across the mote in amazement. Across the mote stood another massive castle just as beautiful as the first. Each year the king would load one boat with all the jewels, silver, and gold it could hold and send it across the mote to the other castle. A second boat would take his daughter across. There she would stand, anxiously waiting to see if any young man were brave enough to accept the king's challenge, and year after year, nothing.

Every year like clockwork, the king would stand on the water's edge and yell to the people, "Is there no one here who will accept my challenge?" Here is where I insert the challenge and the lesson in this chapter. To take his daughter's hand in marriage, and marry into the wealthiest family in the land, one young man would have to swim 300 yards. I must tell you this was no ordinary mote and no ordinary 300-yard swim. The mote was infested with sharks, alligators, piranha, and snakes.

The king issued his challenge again, and still, nothing. The king waited a few minutes longer through the silence and issued his challenge yet a third time and still, all was quiet on the water's edge. The king then turned to his daughter and just when he began to wave her back to the main castle, there was a huge splash! All the town's people turned to see the commotion and to their amazement, there was a young man swimming towards the second castle.

All the town's people started to cheer him on as he swam feverishly. The king cheered, clapped, and whistled the young man on. Halfway to his goal the water began to bubble. The people could see the sharks, alligators, piranha, and snakes closing in from all sides. The young man began to swim faster and, in a flash, he was gone. A calm came over the water and the town's people. On the water's edge were the faint sounds of people murmuring. Blood was visible in the water where the young man went under.

The king kept his eyes on the water dreading the thought that the young man was gone. The whispers and murmurs became louder. Just when all looked lost, the young man popped up gasping for air. The king and the town's people began cheering even louder as the young man swam for his life. This time, he began going under and twirling purposely as he swam to avoid what seemed to be imminent death.

The king and the town's people were in a frenzy cheering the young man on. 100 yards close! 75 yards close! 50 yards close and the young man put his head down and swam for his life! Finally, he was at the water's edge. Exhausted, clothes torn to shreds, and bleeding from head to toe, he dragged himself onto the shore where he collapsed to safety.

The king's daughter ran to him, dropped to her knees, and began hugging, kissing, and holding him in her arms. Fifteen minutes passed and the young man, still exhausted and beaten from the ordeal, mustered the energy to climb to his feet. The King's daughter held him up as they made for the boat. One of the king's guards helped them into the boat and they headed back across the moat towards the main castle. As the boat drew closer, the cheers and screams became louder and louder.

As soon as the boat reached the shore, the king and town's people anxiously waited to greet the brave young man. The town's people cleared a path for the king as he ran to the boat offering the young man his hand. As he helped his daughter and the young man out of the boat, he embraced the young man as if he was his son.

The king was amazed and with a smile from ear to ear, he raised the young man's hand high into the air. The crowd cheered, screaming the young man's name. In disbelief with what he just witnessed, the king began to quiet the crowd.

Standing next to the brave young man with his hand on his shoulder, the king began to shout, "What bravery, what courage, what fearlessness! Ladies and gentlemen and my good towns people, here stands a young man of valor, full of determination and pure guts. What an example of heroism and true grit"! The king then asked the young man a question and silence fell over the crowd.

The king asked the young man what made him decide to jump in and go for it? The young man paused and lowered his head as he collected his thoughts. After a few seconds, the young man, with a look of confusion, lifted his head, shrugged his shoulders, and answered, "I didn't jump. My friend pushed me in."

I bet the answer the young man gave was the furthest thing from your mind. When I first heard the story, I laughed as the ending threw me for a loop, but the lesson was very clear:

When it comes to success, we all need a push.

Success is never a straight line to the top. There will most inevitably be pitfalls. Remember...

life is 10 percent of what happens to us and 90 percent of how we respond to the pitfalls.

We cannot control what happens, but we can control our attitude towards what happens.

If you are to achieve the level of success you want for yourself, you must get in the game! So many people stand on the water's edge of life and they just peer in. The craziest thing is they are literally watching others swim and succeed yet they still choose not to act. You can stand there contemplating life, wishing and hoping things were different, but I can guarantee if you do nothing, nothing is exactly what you will get.

The great hockey hall of famer Wayne Gretzky said you miss 100 percent of the shots you don't take. That statement couldn't be any truer. One of the biggest mistakes anyone can make is thinking or wishing things around us will change. For things to change, you have to change. There are no shortcuts to success. The moat around the castle is the moat and it's never going to change. If you are to be successful you are going to have to work on you. You are going to have to upgrade you and your skill set.

One of my mentors is a motivational speaker and life coach. They call him the Blue-Collar Millionaire. He started his career in law enforcement in California. He knew early on he was destined for greatness. Unfortunately, as a Los Angeles police officer, the day-to-day stress of responding to society's ills became too much. After all, he wasn't being invited to family cookouts when calls came rolling in.

He knew the way to change society was to help as many people as possible find their calling. He had a burning desire to help others achieve success so he did what most wouldn't. He stood on the water's edge of life and jumped in. Today he and his wife are millionaires traveling all over the world helping hundreds of thousands identify their passion. I am proud and elated to say I am one of those people.

One of the most important lessons Dave and his wife Yvette taught me is to understand what we can control and what we cannot control. Too many individuals stress over situations and people. We can't control their thoughts, words, and actions. Situations and people are totally out of our control. Placing energy there is a complete waste of time.

What we can control is how we respond and how we show up. Dave constantly reminds me that showing up is half the battle. The other half of being successful is action. Whenever I feel my business starting to plateau, Dave will tell me without fail, "Show more people." Share your enthusiasm for what you're working on with more people. If you feel your business becoming stagnant, I am telling you to show more people, sit with more people, let more people see what you're passionate about. If you are not where you want to be in life, I can tell you with almost complete certainty, action cures all.

> *The opposite of*
> *action is inaction,*
> *and inaction is the*
> *cousin of mediocrity.*

How do the most successful stay motivated when most struggle to maintain a consistent level of excitement? It's the push! The king asked the young man's friend why in the world would you push your friend into what seemed like eminent peril? The young man's friend responded...

> ***"I didn't push him into peril, I pushed him into his greatness!"***

Sometimes people see things in us we don't see in ourselves. The only way you will truly be successful is getting out of your comfort zone and taking some risk.

I am sure at some point in your life you've heard someone tell you, "no risk, no reward," right? In order to be successful, you must have skin in the game. I am baffled by the number of people I have met who have the most elaborate dreams but aren't willing to sacrifice to make them a reality. They want everything but they're not willing to sacrifice anything. They play it safe.

You can choose to play it safe and there is nothing wrong with that decision. If you do, you are amongst 95 percent of the country. Only a few will ever feel what complete freedom looks and feels like. The freedom to do what you want, when you want, where you want, with whom you want, for as long as you want, no matter the cost. That's my definition of freedom and in order to attain it, you have to be willing to jump, find someone willing to push you, sacrifice and never quit.

Here's what I know:
Success will NEVER
bend to NO SACRIFICE.
The most successful people
on earth had to make
incredible sacrifices to
achieve their level
of success.

Here's another thing I know: They jumped in or they were pushed in. They may have jumped in on their own but we all still need a push from time to time. My push comes in the form of mentors who see the greatness inside of me.

I have mentors to this day who push me to be the best version of myself. Their perspective (OPP) is invaluable. If you are humble enough to allow someone to help guide you with your journey, it can be extremely rewarding. Earlier in life I was the guy who thought he knew it all. I felt my way was the right way because for the most part, that way of thinking served me pretty well.

Later I realized that way of thinking only allowed me to

get so far. I was my own worst enemy and didn't even know it. Only when I started investing in personal development did I realize my full potential.

Personal development is a never-ending process. You must become vigilant in your quest to be better. The process to develop oneself is no different from the work athletes put in to become great. You have to create a winning workout regimen. Decide what it is you are willing to commit too.

For me, I started reading 10 pages a day. Although audiobooks would have been easier, easier wouldn't have challenged me and held me accountable. Again, I began this journey to be better and to do so I had to get out of my comfort zone.

Getting comfortable being uncomfortable is something you are going to have to consider doing daily if you are to be successful. I wish I had someone to tell me the importance of personal development at an earlier age. I wish I were given a book like this to guide me. If I had mentors like I do today and were introduced to personal development, I genuinely believe I would have played division one basketball. I believe I would have created a much bigger brand as Dj Finesse, and I know I would have been able to make a much bigger impact sooner.

If you are lucky enough to find a mentor or someone willing to invest in you and push you to be the best version of yourself, embrace that opportunity. They may know something you don't and when they give you that push, don't resist. Instead, swim as hard as you can toward your goals. No matter what obstacles stand in your way, have faith. Attack them with courage and remain disciplined. Know that success is never easy but when you get to the shore and look back at your journey, it will be well worth the pain and sacrifice.

TAKEAWAYS

Who sees the greatness in you? Who can you lean on when times get tough? Who is willing to push you towards your greatness and wants nothing in return? What sacrifices will you make to achieve your goals? Try to recall situations in your life that required you to decide. How did you respond, and did you get the desired outcome? After reading this chapter, ask yourself if you would respond differently to those situations. Jot down your thoughts and takeaways in the space provided below.

CHAPTER 5

A CHANGE
GON' COME

As I write this chapter, I hope you will relate to the stories I share. A lot of what I have learned has come from past experiences growing up as I have mentioned earlier. I have been fortunate enough to connect with some amazing people who have become mentors. They continue to pour into me in an effort to push me to be the best version of myself. Although they came later in life, I am forever grateful they came, so understand it's never too late to grow.

Everyone wants to be successful. If you ask 1,000 people to explain their idea of success and the dream life they wish for themselves, you will get 1,000 different definitions.

Success is a relative term and everyone's definition reflects the needs and wants of each person.

Everyone's journey from where they are in life, to where they want to go is vastly different. Ironically, when we talk about the American dream, most will paint a picture of a mansion, yacht, and a luxury vehicle. Who am I to tell you that picture isn't worth painting? There's absolutely nothing wrong with knowing what you want in life. We live in the richest country in the world. If that's your idea of success, rock on and go for it because it's more than possible.

What you need to understand is the "what" and "how" to get there. "What" will you do that will give you the life of your dreams, and "how" will you go about achieving it? There is a huge disparity of wealth in this country. According to the Washington Post the top 20% have amassed the majority of the country's wealth and the gap between the HAVEs and the have NOTs continues to widen.

Most of us have big dreams but haven't found the vehicle that can get us to our desired destinations. I continually speak with people and the first question I ask is, *how are you doing?* I am genuinely interested in seeing how life is. I am also interested in seeing what life is not. Without fail, 95% of the people give me the following responses:

"It is what it is" - What they're really saying is they've finally given up. This is all life has to offer so I might as well just accept it.

"Taking it day by day" - This tells me you are in a vicious cycle with everyday being the same. You haven't formulated a real plan that can give you some different choices for your life.

"On my grind" - This tells me that life is a struggle and they haven't quite gotten it figured out.

"Just trying to keep my head above water" - This tells me they are living check to check and are in survival mode. This is where people become desperate.

I can count on one hand the number of times I have heard someone respond to my question with, "Life is great," or "I am doing phenomenal." That was truly troubling. Why are so many people living uninspired? Why are the vast majority of people I come across living unfulfilled lives? If this is you, know *a change gon' come* if you want it, but you have to really want it.

Why do I know this to be true, you might ask? These were my responses years ago when someone asked me how I was doing. I write this because I am not exempt from the struggle. When the economy took a dip in 2008-09 the struggle was real and not just for me; the majority of the country felt it.

I remember it like it was yesterday. My wife and I had

been talking about career paths. It seemed like every six months she would get this glazed look in her eyes. I knew at that moment she was no longer excited about her job. Every six months like clockwork we would sit and talk about the different careers she might want to explore and without fail, she would respond that she's always had an interest in nursing. Of course I wanted to support her dream and passion as she did mine. I told her as long as she settled, she would never be satisfied. I say this to you as well. How many of you are truly living the dreams you once had as a child? Conversely, how many of you are simply conforming to what society has handed you? At some point in time you have to put yourself first.

How many of you have taken a flight on an airplane? No matter the airline, during every flight the crew covers the airplane's safety regulations and passenger protocol in case of an emergency. During their instructions they go over what to do in case of a loss in cabin pressure. They show every passenger how to put on their oxygen masks and without fail, they instruct adults to secure their masks first then help the children.

Going after the goals and dreams in your heart is much the same.

In order for you to help others, you have to first make sure your foundation is secure.

A drowning person has no chance in saving a drowning person. Someone has to get to dry land and then throw the lifeline.

At the time my wife and I were planning her new career move, I was self-employed as a Dj towards the end of my career. Money was fairly good but not enough to sustain the household and she knew it. If her becoming a nurse was going to work, she would have to go to school full time. To do so, that meant forfeiting a lot of income. Remember I said earlier success will NEVER bend to no sacrifice and boy did we sacrifice!

Have you heard the biblical phrase, "Pride comes before the fall" (Proverbs 16:18)? The verse states, "pride goeth before destruction, and haughty spirit before a fall. Yea, all of you be subject one to another, and be clothed with humility: for God resists the proud, and giveth grace to the humble." You can't be so proud that you only do things for your benefit. God gives grace to those of us humble enough to put our pride aside to clothe or help others in time of need.

This was a gut check time. Every ounce of me wanted to stay self-employed as a Dj. I hated the idea of going back to a 9 to 5 job after basking in the splendor of independence. I remember my cousin Neal always used to say, "Pride used the wrong way is a dangerous tool." This was bigger than me. This was my wife and I thought about all the days she held down the home while I was out creating my Dj brand.

Our son at the time was 8 and our daughter was away in college. I couldn't in good consciousness ask her to hold down the fort at home and go to school full time while I was running the streets from club to club. I decided to swallow my pride and go back to a 9 to 5 to help get her through school.

How many of you would make the same decision? What are you willing to do in order for things to change?

> *Life does not give you*
> *what you want... it gives*
> *you who you are.*

Look at where you are currently and look back on your last 3 years. Are you in the same place or worse? Are things getting better or are they status quo? Have you made any changes to your current lifestyle? If not, you are exactly where you are supposed to be. Remember, one of the biggest mistakes people make is thinking that at some point in time things will miraculously get better without them changing a thing. That way of thinking is truly the definition of insanity.

Try this for 30 days. Pay for a gym membership of your choosing. Walk through the door each of those 30 days, stand there for 5 minutes, look around and walk out. At the end of 30 days look at yourself in the mirror and report your results. If you are expecting 6-pack abs and the physique of your dreams, pinch yourself and wake up.

> ### *In order for things to change you are going to have to work on yourself.*

Just walking through the door of the gym isn't enough. You are going to have to get on the exercise bike of life. You are going to have to curl books like you would weights. You are going to have to attend personal development seminars like you would a spin class.

Like an intense workout, halfway through her schooling it became financially unbearable. Living check to check would have been a welcomed blessing. We were living credit card to credit card. My wife was working in transport at a hospital in Rhode Island. She started in transport to get her foot in the door of one of the most prestigious women's hospitals in New England.

One evening I was sitting on the couch watching television as she was working second shift. As I sat watching television, I began seeing flashing lights coming through our blinds. I didn't pay it any attention as I assumed it was a rescue or utility truck going down our street. After a few minutes with the lights still flashing through the blinds, I began hearing this distinct beeping sound. It was the sound you hear when a truck is backing up. I decided to get up and peer through the blinds. To my surprise, I noticed a tow truck backing up towards the front of our car. I immediately jumped up, put my sneakers on and ran outside. My intent was to somehow talk the gentleman out of towing our car.

To say it was a quick conversation is an understatement. He told me he was simply doing his job and that he had orders to repossess our car for non-payment. As I write this, know that it's still difficult to talk about because it brings me back to that moment where things were uncertain at best.

A range of emotions came over me. I stood there talking to myself, asking how in the hell did we get here? Was I failing my family? After all it was my job to provide for them. I started to doubt myself and my purpose. I started looking back on all the decisions that led me to this point. Was I a failure or did I just fail to plan correctly?

I realize now that
no one plans to fail,
we simply fail to plan.

As people, we've become accustomed to doing the same thing over and over. We do it without question and all too often without thought. Our days have become almost ritualistic with no variation. At that moment in time, this was me.

I called my wife and let her know what was happening. Understand, we weren't driving a Beamer, Benz, or Bentley. It was a Nissan Sentra! I said to myself, *have things gotten so bad that we can no longer afford a Nissan Sentra?* Obviously yes. She began to explain in her soft broken voice that she didn't have the heart to tell me we were late on payments and could no longer afford the car.

At that moment I made a decision. I had to start looking for new opportunities. If I kept doing what I was doing, I was going to keep getting what I was getting. If you've been in a situation similar to ours, know you don't have the luxury of being broke and skeptical. So many people I come across are struggling to make ends meet yet they aren't willing to look at anything different or take any risk. I am here to tell you, you have to have skin in the game.

> *You have to take calculated risk or risk staying exactly where you are in life.*

We live in the richest country in the world. There are opportunities all around you if you genuinely want change. I am sure you've heard the phrase, no risk, no reward, haven't you?

Are you willing to risk who you are for who you want to become?

If you don't get anything else from this chapter, I hope you at least understand that concept. In order to be successful, you are going to have to reprogram your thinking. Most of us have been conditioned to protect scarcity. Have you ever seen someone hover over his or her food? They literally wrap their arms around their plate in protection mode.

In most cases there is always enough food for all, but because of past experiences, their default response is to hover over their food even when there is no real threat. What are you so vehemently protecting? What are you so afraid of losing? These were the tough conversations I had to have with myself. These are the tough conversations I want you to have with yourself.

I needed to be brainwashed. I needed to wash my brain of all the negative talk, all the negative thoughts that weren't serving me. I advise you to do the same. I had to condition myself to believe this was not the life that was intended for us to live. I advise you to do the same! Remember, in my mind I was still Dj Finesse, a former Dj for Bad Boy records; the guy everyone thought had it all figured out. I can tell you everything that glitters isn't gold.

I had to realize where I was in life and what I did in the past couldn't get me where I wanted to go. If you believe what I am telling you and you begin to approach situations differently, a change gon' come!

Looking back, I wished I realized the bottom doesn't have to fall out in order for you to wake up. If you are reading this book, use these stories to inspire you to act now. Please understand that something tragic does not have to happen in order for you to change your situation. Change can also occur during positive phases of one's life.

I heard the great Les Brown deliver a speech where he asked the audience, "What is the benefit in waiting to act?" Time is the most precious commodity that too many of us waste. I realized I had to act with urgency. Our situation required that kind of response. Now I act out of purpose. My mentor Dave Ulloa, who I mentioned in a previous chapter, asked, "When would now be a good time to do something different?"

Unfortunately, most, like me, will wait until the bottom falls out to act. I am here to tell you this does not have to be the case. As people, we all have greatness inside of us. No one was born without a purpose. You were designed to win but programmed to lose. We have been taught to be reactive instead of proactive. That type of mindset can create a sense of desperation.

When we act out of desperation, what choices do we

have? My question to you is this: If the choices offered during desperate times were choices that could really enhance your quality of life, wouldn't you have engaged in them long before desperate times? You would never choose those options because they didn't seem viable when things were good. They only seem viable in times of complete chaos. Chances are, you, again like me in that time of my life, believe you have limited options and that is the furthest from the truth.

Opportunities that can add value to your life and the lives of others are in abundance, but you have to recognize they exist. If you miss your window, remember no opportunity is wasted. My wife saw an opportunity to change her life and by acting on her passion, it changed the financial landscape of our family. Please believe it wasn't easy but if you ask her, it was well worth it.

I saw her grow through the process of becoming a nurse. Again, are you willing to sacrifice who you are for who you want to become? I saw her push herself like I have never seen before. There were times she wanted to quit. She would literally cry in my arms and tell me she couldn't do it anymore.

Time and time again we banded together as a family and helped her push through. She needed "the push." No shortcuts, no easy route, no cheating. Just courage, hard work, dedication, sacrifice, a lot of tears and a burning desire to reach her goal.

Today she is a registered nurse. She is in upper management at the same hospital where she started in transport. She has her bachelor's degree and is taking courses towards her master's degree. You too have this greatness inside you.

> *Know that your "why"*
> *will create your way!*
> *When the reason you do what*
> *you do is bigger than you,*
> *you can become unstoppable.*

I decided to follow her lead and go back to school to get my degree. Why? As I look back at my family, I realized a pattern. My mom was an amazing tennis player in high school and had a scholarship to Michigan State. She forfeited that scholarship and married my dad. My mom did take a few college courses but never got her degree. In the beginning of this book I gave you a snapshot into my dad's life, so you know my dad never attended college.

My brother was an amazing basketball talent. After graduating high school, he attended the Community College of Rhode Island where he earned a division 2-basketball scholarship to Bryant College. After 1 year, his grades slipped, and he was forced to leave school. He landed at

Rhode Island College where he would play another year before leaving again. He, like my mom, didn't finish college.

My cousin to this day is one of the best female basketball players I have ever seen. She went to Central High School in Providence Rhode Island in the early 80's. There she became a McDonald's All-American. That meant she was one of the top 24 female basketball players in the country. She had scholarship offers from every major division one university in the country and ended up choosing the University of Maryland.

She, like my mom, and brother didn't finish college. Another cousin of mine went to the University of Connecticut and she, like my mom, brother, and first cousin, didn't finish college. I had yet another cousin who went to the University of Rhode Island and was literally 2 classes from finishing his bachelor's degree. He was actually allowed to walk on stage with an agreement that he would complete the 2 required courses over the summer. He, like my mom, brother, and 2 other cousins never finished college.

I am wondering if you are starting to see the pattern. No, let me add another. My daughter attended the University of Rhode Island and she, like me, my mom, brother, and 3 cousins didn't finish college. Every person I mentioned is my family and are great people who I love dearly. This has nothing to do with who they are and the success they have all achieved. This part of the chapter is a lesson about identifying and being brave enough to face and break patterns so a change will come.

I promised my parents when I left college to pursue music, I would get my degree and now was the time. The bottom had fallen out financially. We just filed for bankruptcy and I hadn't found anything that could make our situation better. I realized our son was next in line to go to college and not finish if the pattern held true.

I remember hearing in my head the voices of my parents telling me what most parents tell their children. In order to be successful, you have to go to college, get good grades so you can get a good job. Have any of you heard that before? Given the current circumstances, all roads lead to me going back to college.

I noticed the pattern of my family. We were an extremely talented bunch of people who didn't finish college. If family cycles were a real thing, our son was next in line to start and never finish college. The thought of that was disturbing. I have no idea why I didn't see it sooner, especially with our daughter, but there it was staring me in the face. We only know what we know, right?

When you're faced with obstacles, what is your response? How do you handle them? No matter the journey, obstacles are going to be a part of it. The better prepared, the better equipped you will be to handle adversity when it shows up.

I began thinking, how unfair would it be to put the pressure of breaking our family's cycle on our son? I am sure he had no idea the cycle existed, but I did, and that was all I needed to move into action. At 40 I made the jump to go back to Rhode Island College to earn my degree in Criminal Justice. I didn't just earn it, I crushed it by making the Dean's List every semester.

I remember graduation day like it was yesterday. I was so proud to have my entire family in attendance. My parents, my wife, my brother and his family, my daughter, son, and in-laws were all in the crowd. I specifically remember our son having a huge AAU tournament I felt he needed to attend but he opted not to go. He told me he needed to be there to see me cross the stage. It was so fitting to have my parents and our kids in attendance because they were my "why". When the graduation ceremony was finished, I was at a loss for words. Tears of joy and accomplishment streamed down my face. It was one of the proudest moments in my life. Of course, finishing what I started is extremely important but what was more important is *why* I finished.

I fulfilled a promise I made to my parents. I felt a huge sense of pride knowing what I had just accomplished. This wasn't just my diploma; this was our family's diploma, and no one could take that away. The cycle had been broken and I knew from this point on *a change gon' come!*

Is this starting to sink in? Are these stories and lessons

helpful? Everything I write is for you. I believe we all have an incredible opportunity to turn our tests into testimony. If what I am saying resonates deep inside, it's because I have struck an emotional chord with you. You too have a story. You are creating it every day through your personal experiences. Know everything you go through is for a reason and nothing just happens. What you do with it is entirely up to you. When you decide quitting is not an option and push through the fear, the anxiety, or whatever is holding you back from greatness, that's where the growth happens.

It's in adverse times that the mind becomes extremely creative and begins to establish an alternate route to the destination you desire. Believe in yourself and that you are more resilient than you think. Trust the process and I guarantee *a change gon' come!*

TAKEAWAYS

If you were to ask the people closest to you, would they say you've changed, and is that change for the better? How have you grown from year to year? Look back and try to identify patterns, behaviors, and cycles that may exist within your family. How are they serving you and what is the benefit of NOT letting go of things and people that are negatively impacting your life? Change happens in the brave moments of self-reflection. Attempting to identify your "why" will clear the way. Who do you want to become and who is stopping you? Use the space provided below to jot down your takeaways from this chapter.

_____

_____

_____

_____

_____

_____

_____

_____

_____

_____

_____

_____

_____

_____

_____

_____

_____

CHAPTER 6

OLD LIFE

I don't believe you have to have formal training to speak from the heart. People resonate with honesty and transparency. To this point I have done my best to lay it all on the line for you hoping my lessons will help you create lessons of your own.

You don't have to be a great lecturer or writer to be the light others need. Your story, if you choose to tell it, can help people emerge from some of the darkest places in their lives. This level of thinking and consciousness was foreign to me until this point.

This will be a chapter that relates to the previous. If you read chapter 5, you know I mentioned that *A Change Gon' Come*. If you follow what I believe to be sound advice, change will indeed happen. Conversely, the change that happens may not come in the package you designed for yourself as I also mentioned earlier. I believe all the chapters have useful information but if there is one chapter that pinpoints exactly what happens when you're trying to get from where you are to where you want to go, this is it!

The day I walked across the stage during my college graduation ceremony, I was on an all-time high. A new world had just opened, as I finally made good on my promise to my parents that I would get my degree. I closed the chapter on our family's legacy of not finishing what we started. The cycle had finally been broken and things couldn't be better. I had that piece of paper and an accomplishment that no one could ever take from me. The question then became how would I go about monetizing my degree? How would this new chapter in my life play out? What was my profession going to be?

I was eager to enter into the workforce and see how life would be different with a degree. For the first time in my life I was honestly excited to begin my job search. I had a college degree, and this was my ticket to freedom, so I thought. I began by rewriting my resume and man did it look sexy! It was still surreal looking at the education section as it read, BA in Arts and Sciences with a concentration in Criminal Justice. To this day I smile when I read it.

I began looking for opportunities online. I applied for opportunities I felt matched my interest, skill set, qualifications, and financial demands. I didn't look at any job that paid under $50,000 a year to start. I truly felt this was more than a reasonable starting point given my newly acquired degree and previous work experience. How many of you in the workforce with degrees felt the same when you started applying for jobs in your field of study? How long did that excitement last for you? Mine was short lived!

I applied and applied and applied. Email after email, application after application. I waited and waited. I began to get discouraged when I didn't receive immediate responses, but I remembered hearing my parent's voices in my head as a child. They always told my brother and I that good things come to those who wait. Patiently I kept applying and awaited responses from employers. After a few weeks the emails started to pour in. I thought to myself, finally someone sees my worth. The feeling of importance and value came to a screeching halt when every email read.

Dear Mr. Santos,

We have received your cover letter and resume. Thank you in advance for applying. Although you were a very strong candidate, you were one of many applying for this position. Unfortunately, we have decided to go in a different direction. We will most certainly keep your resume on file for future consideration, blah, blah, blah.

How many of you have gotten an email, or emails, similar to the one I just read? When the first rejection email came in it wasn't really upsetting. I figured at least I was in the game and the game has just begun. After the 9th and 10th emails, I was saying to myself, *this shit is for the birds.* Quitting was not an option, so I pressed on and kept updating my resume to match the opportunity I was applying for. In 6 months, I literally went on 3 job interviews and was turned down for all of them.

I began thinking to myself, what was the value of my degree and how much weight did it really hold? If not for my promise to my parents and my desire to break the family cycle, I would have believed secondary education was a complete waste of my time. Again, how many of you with college degrees reading this feel or felt the same way?

How many of you are working in your field of study being paid your worth? Disheartening isn't it? No worries, this chapter is for you.

What I failed to realize was this was a different day and age. These were different times. A degree that wasn't so common when I was 21 was all too common at 42. Everyone had a degree, or so it seemed. I quickly realized employers weren't going to hire this older gentleman and pay him $50k to start when they could pay $30k to a 24-year-old fresh out of college. Frustration set in and everyone around me could feel it. To say I was jaded was putting it nicely. It occurred to me that I might need more education to secure a career that paid money I would be comfortable making.

Reluctantly, I decided to go back to school to get a master's degree. Let me explain my mindset at that moment in time.

> *I was ok with creating*
> *a comfortable situation*
> *and I was willing to pay*
> *more money for it.*

How many of you have become complacent? How many of you tell yourselves you just want to be comfortable and pay the bills? I ask that because that was exactly where I was heading, and I had no idea. Higher education equaled more student loans and didn't guarantee a job in my field, or rate of pay that matched my talents, experience, and qualifications. I began thinking to myself, *why would anyone pay more for something that wasn't already working? Was I brainwashed? Was I ignoring the numbers?* I started doing some research about college degrees. What I found was totally contradictory to what I was sold. Yes "sold" and not "told." *I was sold on the idea that a college degree meant freedom.* Life with a degree would give you everything you needed to be successful in every sense of the word. What I found was shocking to say the least.

I started researching information on the national college dropout rate. I found 33% of students earn a college degree in four years. What happens to the other 67%? 57.6% earn their degree in six years. What happens to the other 43%?

At private colleges and universities, the four-year graduation rate is 52.8% with 65.4% earning a degree in six years. What about the other 48% and 35%? If a high school graduated only 33% of its students in four years, it would be shut down or taken over by the state immediately. Imagine a high school having to give students two more years to get their high school diploma and make you pay for it. Yet still, after six years 43% still don't finish! This was astonishing information. I was caught in the system of believing education equaled freedom.

It pains me to write this but in order for you to get the lesson, I have to be transparent. I didn't know it, but I was settling. In that period of my life I was ok looking for opportunities that would allow me to be mediocre at best. Understand I am not anti-college. *I am simply stating too many of you have talents and interests that need to be explored and the answer isn't always college.* Identify your passion. Answer your true calling and educate yourselves in that field. Find what it is you love and become the best at it.

I will illustrate the point of the previous paragraph with a real example from a student teacher interaction in my high school. I am a Behavior Specialist in our local high school and one day as I was sitting at my desk, a student came into my classroom and was upset that a teacher told the entire classroom that without a college degree, they wouldn't amount to anything.

I immediately told her what I tell all of my students. Don't raise your voice, improve your argument. I advised her to go to the Internet and research successful people without college degrees and report back to me. She made a list for the teacher and me. I'd advise you to do the same if you haven't already. Print it out and post it to your vision board.

Her list included:

Bill Gates
(Microsoft, net worth $107.1 billion)

Mark Zuckerberg
(Co-founder of Facebook, net worth $72.1 billion)

Richard Branson
(Virgin Group, net worth $4 billion)

Jay-Z
(Hip Hop artist / net worth 1 Billion)

Ellen DeGeneres
(Dropped out after 1 semester, net worth $450 million)

Ted Turner
(Founder CNN, net worth $2.2 billion)

Anna Wintour
(Vogue Magazine, net worth 35 million)

Larry Ellison
(Entrepreneur and philanthropist, net worth $69.3 billion)

Russell Simmons
(Co-founder Def Jam Records, net worth $340 million)

Steve Jobs
(Co-Founder of Apple, net worth at death $21.6 billion)

Michael Dell
(Dell Technologies, net worth $35 billion)

David Geffen
(Asylum Records, net worth $ 8.5 billion)

Kim Kardashian
(Kardashian family, net worth $350 billion)

John D. Rockefeller
(Oil tycoon, net worth at time of his death $340 billion)

Sean "Puffy" Combs
(CEO Bad Boy Entertainment, net worth $740 million)

If you look at this list, there's no doubt these iconic figures are educated. They have mastered their prospective industries, but none needed a college degree to amass their wealth and influence. I am sure the teacher was giving the student advice she believed would serve her in the future. But she, like most, only knows what she knows.

I would suggest to anyone reading this book to start looking at things differently. The information I am giving you is the information I had to use in order to get to this place in life. This is not hypocrisy. I am not telling you one thing and doing another. This is personal experience I believe that has helped me immensely and here's another example.

One day I was headed to Dj a celebrity golf tournament and an email popped up on my cell phone. At the time of the email I was still in my job search phase. I opened the email and saw it was an opportunity to work at a small charter school in Providence. Ironically, I was very familiar with the school. It was known to be one of the highest achieving schools in the city. It boasted a 92% graduation rate. I was eager to be a part of their success and I loved the idea of being able to positively impact the lives of young people. What I wasn't excited about was the rate of pay.

How many of you are in jobs or careers that pay the bills but not your worth? How many of you are excited to be in your field and actually love what you do? I don't know about you, but I was banging my head against the wall in frustration.

As a side note it was so hard for me to come back to the 9 to 5 life after being self-employed. Once you get that taste of what it's like to own your own time, giving that up feels like a death sentence. I was never good at being told what to do, when to do it and not being paid my worth but there I was.

Know that any time we accept a position in any company in any field, your value is determined by the rate of pay you agree to accept. The minute you sign on that dotted line, you have indirectly told your employer your worth.

I had no idea how much I was devaluing myself. As I sat at my desk pondering my future, I still believed aside from being self-employed, education was the answer to our financial problems. I wasn't ready to commit to the idea that being successful does not necessarily mean you have to have a college degree. I will restate my previous thought. You need to be educated. Being successful does not necessarily mean you need a college degree.

When it came to establishing myself in the 9 to 5 sector, I still believed if I put my head down and grinded long enough, the life I wanted for my family and I was well within reach. After all I was working in academia and every conversation amongst teachers centered on the importance of a college degree.

I began actively looking for a master's degree program. I landed on the campus of Providence College. I knew deep inside I wanted to live a life of purpose. I wanted to be a servant leader, but I wasn't sure what that looked like and how to go about it. I began taking classes towards a Master's Degree in Urban Education with a concentration on teaching African American history.

The first year breezed by and I did exceedingly well. I was into my second year and while still holding down the job at the charter school, I started to see the politics within the educational system. Too often I saw how the infrastructure of urban education inadequately prepared our youth for the future. I saw a content driven focus that didn't relate to the population being served. Social promotion ran rampant and a true lack of accountability.

As I dug deeper, I realized a grading system that blurred the lines. A lot of students I became extremely close to were coming back reporting how they were not prepared for college. Many students left college and became a part the 43% I spoke of earlier. Others transferred to schools that appeared to have less academic rigor. Was this the system I was paying money to become a part of? I questioned how many teachers knew what was happening and simply turned a blind eye. Or, maybe they honestly believed they were doing some good?

This is by no means an attack on any teacher. I have met some incredibly smart, dedicated, and caring teachers who would do anything for their students. Maybe they came into teaching with high expectations and like me fell victim to the system.

Conformity is the thief of creative expression.

When you conform, you lose sight of what's important to you. I have never been one to conform. I was the complete opposite. Jay-Z said in reference to his career in a song called "Renegade" featuring Eminem, "I drove by the fork in the road and went straight." That was and still is me to this day.

I needed to know my role would be impactful. I needed a platform that allowed me to express what I have learned in an attempt to help students and people in general become the best version of themselves. I was committed and in order to be effective I had to be real and honest with myself.

Students for the most part are razor sharp. They can smell bullshit a mile away. Something resonated deep inside. It didn't feel right. I refused to put my name on anything I didn't believe in. My gut has always served me in the past and I wasn't about to turn from it now. With six classes to go I walked out of Providence College and the master's degree program.

This decision had nothing to do with Providence College, as it is an amazing educational institution. This was my feeling towards the system of education I couldn't see myself becoming a part of. I can hear the chirping as you read this. Why not finish, you ask?

If I am being honest, at the time, part of me felt like I should finish for the sake of finishing what I started. But as you read on you will see exactly why my decision to leave school made perfect sense. I have absolutely no reservations about my decision to leave. A new life was about to emerge, and the old life was about to be a distant memory. I had no idea it was coming, and it came like a thief in the night!

I remember it like it was yesterday. It was Saturday, March 5, 2015. I was sitting in my car and our son was getting his haircut at the Atomic Salon in East Providence, Rhode Island. I was on the phone handling some Dj business and an incoming call showed up and it read Rob

Cappuccilli. I have to give you the back-story on Rob and I so you understand why I answered his call the way I did. What he said to me in that moment and what was to come after has forever changed my life.

At the moment of the call, Rob and I had known each for over 20 years. Rob was remarkably successful in running, owning and operating nightclubs and restaurants. If there was an event he was putting on, I was the first Dj he'd call. We did some amazing events in the past. We always made money and he was always good at paying me what we previously discussed.

Rob and I also dabbled in Network Marketing. We were involved with a company whose product was a juice designed to help boost the immune system and help rid the body of toxins.

Prior to getting involved with the company, I tried the juice and saw firsthand the physical benefits. Again, for me to be a part of anything, it has to resonate deep within, or I'd have no interest. With that being said, I jumped on board. The first 8 months things went really smooth until 2008-2009 when the economy took a dip.

I found it really difficult to share a concept when people could barely pay their mortgage or rent. Our businesses began to suffer and before it bottomed out, we both opted out. This was my second Network Marketing Company. Although I have always made money, I vowed never to do

MLM again if it were product based. I am a true believer in Multi-level Marketing if you find the right company with the right product, platform, business model and leadership.

Because of MLM I now understand leverage and the power of residual income. What I didn't realize as I started in MLM is, people are product and brand loyal. If you don't believe me, try getting a Coca-Cola drinker to drink Pepsi or vice versa. It'd be like pulling teeth. People are creatures of habit. I have a friend of mine who refuses to wear Adidas. He is Nike brand loyal. He is so loyal to Nike; he won't allow his kids to wear anything else.

When Rob called, it had been a couple of years since he and I last spoke. When the phone call came in, I was laughing to myself looking at his name flashing. I knew it was one of two things. He was either calling because he opened a new club or restaurant, or he was calling me about another MLM opportunity.

I answered and said, "Rob I am not buying or selling anything!" I didn't say hello, what's up, long time no see, how's the family, nothing! There is no doubt he heard the conviction in my voice because what he said to me caught me totally off guard.

He made sure I didn't get in another word. With excitement and urgency in his voice of a person who just won the lottery he said, "Mase, it's Capp. Listen, I found water in the desert!" He stopped me dead in my tracks because I was dead set on not wanting to hear any sales pitch. I asked him what the hell he was talking about and he repeated himself, "I found water in the desert!"

Again, I asked, "What the hell are you talking about with this water in the desert bullshit!" He started telling me how he found a way where we could have more fun, travel the world, help a lot of people and if we wanted, we could create another stream of income. I said, "Come again," and he repeated what he said he found.

My antennas were all the way up! Ironically, little did he know how I felt about where I was in life and that I was searching for something? I didn't know what it was exactly, but I knew it wasn't education and teaching. I was more than lacking enthusiasm about my future in education.

It's funny as I look back on that conversation, I remember tuning him out and all I could hear in my head was who the hell wouldn't want to have more fun in their lives? Who wouldn't want to travel the world? Who wouldn't want to be more impactful and help more people? God knows the world needs more people willing to put others before themselves. Lastly, who's not open to possibly making another stream of income? As those thoughts ran through my mind. What he said took seconds but seemed like hours.

I knew by all the traveling I did as a Dj, the enormity of the travel space. I also knew I was looking for a platform to be impactful. I still had the entrepreneur spirit so if there was a way to create another stream of income, I was all in! To say he had my attention would be an understatement!

If this mix of fun, travel, helping people and money were a cocktail, this is a drink I believed the entire bar would be ordering. As my thoughts faded and his voice became clearer, I told him he had 5 minutes to explain what he had found.

He began telling me about this Network Marketing Company that was going to disrupt the travel space. He laid out the company history, purpose, and vision for the future. At first it sounded too good to be true, but as he continued painting the vision of the company and how we fit in, I couldn't help but feel this was it!

This was the opportunity of a lifetime. It was the feeling I had only two other times in my life. I knew when it was the right time to walk away from my first 9-5 job and pursue music full time. I also knew in the core of my soul when it was time to ask my wife for her hand in marriage.

I believe God works in mysterious ways and he makes no mistakes. When you ask, he delivers! I wasn't content with where I was in life and in my occupation. Although I hadn't physically walked away from Providence College at this point, emotionally, it was a forgone conclusion that this was not the path I wanted to pursue.

In my heart I couldn't commit, and I believe God knew it. I am not telling you who or what to believe in. That slippery slope is for someone else to slide down. I can only be transparent and tell you what happened from firsthand experience.

> *When one door closes,*
> *you have to believe*
> *another is sure to open.*
> *The problem most have*
> *is they don't recognize*
> *the opportunity because*
> *it does not look like*
> *what they envisioned.*

Remember as I stated earlier in the book, opportunities are never wasted; they simply go to the next person willing to act. Have you ever had what you believed to be an amazing idea and for some reason you chose not to act on it, only to find out someone else created what you didn't? Opportunities are never wasted.

> *A great idea is only as*
> *great as the person willing*
> *to put their idea into action.*

What was really cool was Rob wasn't alone on the phone when he called. I mentioned in my acknowledgments the role Max Lora played in me writing this book. Max was also in the entertainment industry. He had his own marketing and graphics company. He did most of the graphics for the mix tapes I was putting out and was instrumental in helping format Mixtape Magazine.

When Rob called, I had no idea Max was on the phone. He was the direct link between Rob and I in this company. I had some questions I needed answered but honestly, I was already in. Max answered every question and after 30 minutes on the phone I jumped all in without seeing a thing.

How many of you would have done the same? How many of you are willing to invest in your future and take some risk? I am baffled at the scores of people who are just existing and not living life to it's fullest extent.

When I speak with people about goal setting and their plans for the future, 95% have no idea what the future will look like. As I sit with people, I realize my responses to their struggles can be a bit harsh, but they will always be 100% real.

I have a statement I live by. When speaking with people I always tell them to be careful what you ask for. If you ask me a question, know you are going to get one of two answers; one you like or one you dislike. Which one you get depends on where you are in life?

If you are honest about your current situation and you desire change, it will be a response you like, you embrace, and one that moves you to action. If you're in denial, it will most likely be a response you don't like that will keep you stagnant. The old life will only become a distant memory when you decide to take on something new.

TAKEAWAYS

Think about a time in your life where you've had what looked to be an amazing opportunity and chose not to act on it. Have you ever thought about how different life could be? The goal is to identify what's holding you back from taking action and correct the behavior? Understand your old way of thinking will only get you more of the same. Use the lines provided on the next page and write a list of opportunities you've missed. Next to it, write the reason you chose not to act. If you're honest with yourself, a pattern should emerge. When you see the pattern staring you in the face, have the courage to act on changing it, you deserve it!

_____

_____

_____

_____

CHAPTER 7

THE AWAKENING

*If you want to see
your future, look at
your last five years.*

The decisions you made five years ago determined where you are today. The decisions you make today will determine your next five years. Unfortunately, many of us have been asleep at the wheel. Stop for a minute and think of the route you take home from work. Try to recall a time where you were on the phone driving home but can't remember getting there? Why, might you ask? This is the route we choose to take every day. Absolutely no thought is needed for you to get home. For too many of people, life is much the same. Your journey has become mundane. Life has become stagnant with no thought. It reminds of the movie

Groundhog Day starring Bill Murray. Too many people are living the same day, with each day resembling the last; no variation, purpose or excitement. As you read this chapter, I want you to keep these questions in the back of your mind. When did I stop dreaming? When did I decide the future I designed for myself wasn't attainable?

Let this chapter be your wakeup call. Let this be the moment in your life where you choose a different route. I can promise you your next five years will look exactly the same if you choose to make no changes. Doing nothing is a choice. With that being said, most will choose to do nothing and in my opinion, here's why:

1. *The number one reason people choose not to act and follow their dreams is FEAR!* People fear the unknown. As I mentioned before, people are creatures of habit and change is extremely difficult for so many people.

People have a fear of loss. They often fear losing the very thing that may be holding them back. It may be a friend, family member, loved one or a job.

People fear the thought of rejection. They feel if they don't ask, they can't be rejected, and they are absolutely right. *Again, all I know is you miss 100% of the shots you don't take.* We fear what others think of us, so we put up a facade. Trust me your friends think what they think already, they just haven't the stomach to tell you. Most of us put so much emphasis on what others think that we actually stop thinking for ourselves. I could make a "fear" list as long as the day, but I think you get the point.

I heard two great acronyms for the word **FEAR**: *F*ace *E*verything *A*nd *R*ise or *F*orget *E*verything *A*nd *R*un. Which one you choose is entirely up to you.

2. *People have this fallacy that what they are doing currently will all of a sudden give them the life of their dreams.* Successful people understand the position they're in and how they got there. They also understand in order to move forward and achieve a higher level of success, they are going to have to acquire new skills and do something different.

> *Successful people make decisions based on where they want to go in life. Average people make decisions based on where they are in life.*

Here's my question: if what you were currently doing could create the life of your dreams, wouldn't you already have it? What new skills have you acquired? Who are you listening to? What books are you reading (besides this one) that can help you move into action? Zig Ziglar says, "If you are not willing to learn, no one can help you, if you are determined to learn no one can stop you." This brings us to my third point.

3. *Complacency is the close cousin of mediocrity.* Too many have looked at their lives and decided this is all life is supposed to be. I mentioned earlier the all too common statements of mediocrity. "I just want to be comfortable" is another.

What you are actually saying is "I just want to be average." I hear it all the time and it drives me crazy. If you are waking up every morning looking to be comfortable, you are asking to be average. Again, be careful what you ask for because life will deliver your order swiftly to your table. After a while what I have noticed is people simply decide to give up. Life has pinned them down long enough, so they tap out.

Understand the fight isn't with life the fight is with you. Everything you have or don't have in life is determined by your decisions or indecision. Michael Jackson created a great song called "Man in The Mirror."

If you want change and you're courageous enough, I suggest you ask the man or woman in the mirror before asking me. He/she knows you better than I. I had to have that tough conversation with myself so again this is not information I am telling you to use without first using it myself. Trust me, the future you will thank you for that brave conversation.

4. *Lastly, the fourth reason I believe people aren't living the goals and dreams God placed in their hearts is dishonesty.* Why are we dishonest about where we are in life? The only reason I can think of is PRIDE.

I am not talking about being proud to be an American or being proud to be a person of color. This is not the same as being proud to get my college degree and proud to break a family cycle. I am talking about foolish pride.

To make my point, I created an acronym for what I believe **PRIDE** stands for: **P**eople, **R**eluctantly, **I**ndicate, **D**iscomforting, **E**motions. How honest are you with yourself about where you are in life? Are you too proud to ask for help? Are you too proud to ask the friend or family member you know is successful, how he or she created their success?

Are you quicker to judge another person's success instead of grading your lack of it? Most are too proud to admit failure. I have failed time and time again and that's exactly why I succeed. *Remember there is no such thing as losses, only lessons.* Don't let your stubborn foolish pride be the reason you live a life unfulfilled. The next time you feel too proud to do something, think of the acronym I just created and ask yourself if the discomforting emotions you reluctantly indicate to yourself or someone else is serving you?

The project that was presented to me in 2015 was massive and I knew it. There was no time for foolish pride and no time for fear. I realized both Rob and Max knew a lot of people so for me the most important question I had, had everything to do with timing. Knowing Max was in Florida, I asked Rob who in Rhode Island was working on this project and who did he introduce the concept too?

Rob was like the mayor. He told me I was his second phone call. The surfer's mindset kicked in! Was this a wave I could see forming? Was I going to paddle or just sit on the surfboard? I ran a quick risk versus reward analysis and pulled the trigger.

I was fired up and super excited, I told them I was all in and jumped on board. As I raced home it hit me that I didn't consult with my wife and that made me a bit nervous. Spending money without telling her is something I rarely do, but this was an opportunity to travel the world. The feeling in my gut was telling me this was a shot at true freedom, and I wasn't about to ignore it.

I wasn't nervous about my belief that I could make this

work, I was nervous about her response, as this was my third MLM. Each of the previous companies I joined, she made it clear she wanted no parts of.

The difference was, I felt the other companies offered products and a culture she wasn't sold on putting her name on. This was travel and if my friends were right, I knew she'd be all in. After all, I have always lived by the motto that it's better to ask for forgiveness than permission.

I burst through the door excited and I couldn't have gotten two feet on the ground and the first thing out of her mouth was, "What's this money out of account?" Like a little kid who's heard the question but is trying to buy time to create a better answer I said, "Huh?" She asked me again and all I could say was, "I have no idea?" I tried to explain to her what Rob and Max explained to me and that was an epic fail! She was disgusted that I not only jumped into another MLM, she was upset that I didn't tell her and was making another career move without discussing it with her.

If you have ever been in MLM or have attempted to open, or create your own business, there are a few lessons to learn early on from my story.

The first is making sure you discuss any new endeavor with your significant other prior to jumping on board. You will be better served if you involve them in the process from the beginning. This does not mean they will be on board, but the level of respect you show them by involving them from the onset will allow you to move forward with less push back.

Secondly, no matter what MLM you join, it's always a good idea not to run out and throw up on people. As a rule of thumb, remember not to *TELL* anyone anything until you can *SHOW* him or her everything. This will save you a lot of early headache. Third, you have to know if you take no risk, there will be no reward. You have to have skin in the game!

When you start your own business and you genuinely want it to be a success, you cannot say this is something you want to "try" to do. You have to commit to it. I hear people talk about trying MLM or trying a new business and they give themselves a timetable. All too often I hear people say they will give their new business 6 months to a year, and if it's not profitable they're shutting the doors.

> *Know if you give yourself*
> *a set time to be successful,*
> *you have indirectly given*
> *yourself a quit date.*

This is not the same as goal setting or creating benchmarks. Both are proactive and neither indicate the possibility of opting out. By giving yourself a timed ultimatum for success, psychologically you've already determined the possibility that your new endeavor may not work, and the first sign of trouble you're out the door. Remember success is a marathon not a sprint.

> *So many people sign*
> *up for things and*
> *aren't deeply committed*
> *to the process.*
> *They enjoy the idea*
> *of being successful*
> *but aren't committed*
> *to the sacrifice it*
> *takes to get there.*

The great motivational and inspirational speaker Eric Thomas always says, "Everyone wants to be a beast until it's time to do what beasts do!"

You have to not only commit to the process; you have to commit to finishing! Quitting can become habitual. I have seen so many people start and never finish. Most fail to realize the road to the finish line is often shorter than the road back.

Think about the pain you had to go through to get to this point in your life? If you quit all the pain was for nothing. Are you truly prepared to go back to where you were?

I will illustrate this point by a story I heard told by Napoleon Hill. If you don't know who Napoleon Hill is and being successful in anything is a goal of yours, I urge you to invest in your personal development and look into his library of books. To this day Hill continues to be one of the most beloved motivational authors. Millions of people continue to read his work. His books are considered literary art. Writers, like me, and motivational speakers often cite his work. The story goes as follows and along the way I will stop and ask you questions.

R. U. Darby created amazing wealth in the insurance industry but did so only after learning one of the most important lessons in life; quitters never win, and winners never quit. As I tell the story of Darby's uncle who was struck by the 'gold fever' in the gold-rush days, you will see for yourself the point I need you to understand.

Darby's uncle went west to dig and find gold. He knew if he struck gold (as the phrase goes) life would forever be different. How many of you see or create an opportunity and feel like you've struck gold? He made a decision to "*jump*" (as I have mentioned earlier) and went to work with pick and shovel.

How many of you actually jumped and went "*all in*" on your new project? After weeks of labor, the shiny ore became visible and his hard work paid off. How many of you have had early success in your new business? It gets really exciting when you see your business start to flourish in the beginning stages.

He soon realized he needed machinery to bring the ore to the surface. Making sure no one could see where he was digging, he covered up the mine, retraced his footsteps to his home in Williamsburg Maryland. He told only a few of his relatives and neighbors that he struck gold.

Together, they raised the money needed for the machinery and had it shipped. The uncle and Darby went back to work the mine.

The first car of ore was mined and shipped to a smelter. It was said that the returns proved they had one of the richest mines in Colorado! They felt if they were able to mine a few more cars of ore, the debts would be clear, and then the big profits would come pouring in.

How many of you have engaged in something that has had an immediate positive return? It's easy when everything is going according to plan. How do you show up when things go south? That is the real test of your character.

So down went the drills and to say Darby and his uncle were excited is an understatement! Then, as it always does, something happened. The vein of gold ore disappeared! Remember, anything worth having is not going to be easy. They thought for sure they had the goose that laid the golden egg, but it wasn't to be.

They drilled on, desperately trying to pick up the vein again — all to no avail. Finally, they decided to *throw in the towel*. How many of you have had plateaus in your business? Everything slows down to a crawl and you start to question yourself and your decision? Doubt and fear begin to cloud your mind. Your hopes and dreams fade to black.

> *There will always be a time*
> *where your resolve, patience,*
> *stick-to-itiveness is tested.*
> *Nothing great will come*
> *to you without sacrifice.*

Unfortunately, many of you reading this will still give in like Darby and his uncle. My hope is that my story and the stories of others in this book will lead you to a different outcome.

Darby and his uncle inevitably sold the machinery to a junk man for a few hundred dollars and took the train back home. I mentioned in an earlier section of this chapter that opportunities are never wasted; they simply go to the next person ready, willing, and able to act.

The junk man saw an opportunity and decided to call in a mining engineer to look at the mine and do a little calculating. Who do you call when things go south? Who can you call on that can offer insight and help you problem solve? Who do you know better than you in your industry? Don't be too proud to ask for help.

The engineer advised the junkman that the project had

failed because the owners were not familiar with 'fault lines.' His calculations showed that the vein would be found *just three feet from where the Darby's had stopped drilling!* That is exactly where it was found! According to the story, the junk man took millions of dollars in ore because he knew enough to seek expert counsel before giving up.

Napoleon said...

"No man is ever whipped until he quits in his own mind."

Think about that for one second. Stop right now, close your eyes, and take a deep breath. You may be ready to make the biggest mistake of your life by giving up. Just three feet from where they were drilling laid riches. If they took a step back and thought, "how" do we figure out the issue this story may have a completely different ending?

My mentor Max continues to push me and others to think and problem solve. He always tells me when you ask, "how," the mind goes into solution mode. The brain starts computing options and quitting isn't one of them.

Conversely, when you make a decision to give up, the mind kicks into finality mode. It stops looking for solutions. What are you about to give up on? Have you given your endeavor, your business, your sport, your relationship full attention and cooperation? Have you invested in seeking expert advice or counsel? Are you stopping 3 feet from gold? If you've answered yes to any of these, you're in good company because I have been there too!

I remember my first year playing college basketball. It was pre-season conditioning and our coach told the team to bring running shoes and report to the track. We stretched for 15 minutes and he began putting us through conditioning drills. He was preparing us to be able to run a mile in under six minutes.

A couple of weeks went by and I had had enough. When it came time to run the mile, I decided I wasn't going to do it. In my mind I had already quit. I walked to the bleachers and remember telling the coach I didn't come to run track I came to play basketball. He looked at me and with a confident smirk, grinned and told me, "I knew it, I knew you were a quitter."

Man, that was a blow to my gut and ego. Was he right? Was I the very thing my parents always preached against? Was I close to the finish line and ready to turn back at the first sign of adversity? Was I R.U. Darby's uncle? Was I a quitter?

I looked at the coach and in the moment of truth I got up from the bleachers, tied up my sneakers and ran the mile in under six minutes. All through your life you will be challenged. Situations will arise that are going to test you. Know it's preparation for something greater.

> *I would suggest*
> *not stressing over*
> *things in life you*
> *can't control.*

The challenge is equipping yourself mentally to deal with the roadblocks, pitfalls and obstacles that will most surely show up on your road to success. What decisions do you make for your future when things aren't going as planned? No one said being successful was going to be easy. Whoever told you becoming successful was easy, flat out lied to you.

When you start a new project or business, you have to have conviction. Know what you have your hands on. Know that it can add value to the lives of others, but know you have to finish what you've started. So many people are three feet from living the life of their dreams, but they succumb to the obstacles.

People follow strength. They want to know you're all in if they are going to partner or follow you. They have to believe you are not only going to finish, you are committed to helping them finish.

People aren't buying your product or business... They are buying you!

When Rob and Max called, I didn't join because I bought into the company or its product. I joined because I trusted the both of them. I bought into their vision for the future. I bought their excitement and energy. I joined because they pushed all their cards in! They never once said this was something they were going to try. They insisted they were taking this to the top and offered me an opportunity to do it with them. I trusted two friends who had something I was missing, and I was willing to jump and bet on me.

One thing I want you to understand as you move forward in your business is your decision may not resonate with others. What you see others may not see. You have to have thick skin and never waiver. Quitting is never an option.

When my wife and I sat down and I shared my endeavor with her, she immediately told me to get my money back. Actually, she thought Rob and I had gotten hustled if I am being honest. Those were her exact words. She didn't see what I saw. She wasn't supposed to.

Although we are a couple, her life experiences and mine are separate. Those experiences led us to different interests in life. What interest her might be of no interest to me but it doesn't mean I'm oblivious to her wants and needs.

As a side note, as a spouse of a significant other, I'd advise you to care about what your partner cares about. Be present in the moments where they are most excited, trust me. I may not be interested in what my wife is interested in, but I am interested in my wife and that makes all the difference. That interest will be reciprocated.

Our decisions as I mentioned previously, derive from prior knowledge and experiences. Understand no matter how close you are to someone, that does not mean they will see things the way you do.

> *There's beauty*
> *in acknowledging*
> *and learning*
> *what makes us*
> *different*
> *as people.*

Still, people won't always share your vision and that's perfectly fine. Don't take it personally. This I had to learn. When it came to my new endeavor, I was paddling, and she was sitting on the surfboard.

One thing is for sure: As the naysayers cackle, either you are going to be right or they are!

Nothing makes liars out of more people than success.

I had the woman I loved the most telling me I made a poor decision. I could have easily bought her opinion. As much as I love my wife, I had to ask myself was she qualified to give me advice in the industry I was entering. Hell, I was new to the endeavor and I wasn't qualified to give anyone advice, so I totally understood her apprehension.

How many of you are taking advice or buying the opinions of people not qualified to steer you in the direction of your goals and dreams? Often the people you love are the ones who fail to support your dreams. It may be a parent, family member, best friend, college roommate, girlfriend, boyfriend, husband, or wife. No matter who it is, if you are going to buy their opinions, you had better be ready to buy their life.

What I have come to realize most is, those closest to you who choose not to support you do so for 3 reasons.

1. *They don't support it because they are ignorant to the industry you are entering.* They simply pass judgment without having the proper information. Because they have no interest, they believe you shouldn't either.

You will hear statements like, "Why would you join that", or, "I didn't know you had interest in that field". Most objections to your business come from people wanting you to believe they know what they're talking about.

If you understand this about people and you are all in on your project, you will realize the smarter they try to sound, the more ignorant they become. You are the professional not them so agree to disagree and keep it moving.

2. *They care about you and are trying to protect you from failure.* They project their fear of failure onto you. They make statements like, "I heard those things don't work," or, "one of my other friends tried that and it didn't work out for them." Know they aren't you.

Most have never jumped so their default reaction is to convince you to do the same. They aren't walking in your shoes. Their fear of failure has nothing to do with your success. Thank them for their concern and keep it moving.

3. *Some are jealous of your courage to start something new.* They will never say it to your face, but you will often hear it from the rumor mill. Instead of supporting and encouraging your new project, you will hear statements like, "I wouldn't do that if I were you," or, "why would he/she leave their job to pursue that?"

Some truly hope your endeavor does not work because where you succeed shows others where they've failed. After all, they were given the same opportunity and chose not to act. Again, don't give it your energy and keep it moving.

My wife and I were co-creating our future and as much as I respected her opinion, I knew like I mentioned in the earlier paragraph, either she was going to be right or I was. If I were right, life for us would forever be different. I had no idea what my new endeavor would bring for our family and even more for me as a person.

It didn't take long for me to see what Max and Rob saw. On the surface this was an opportunity to travel the world and create memories that would last a lifetime. Beneath it laid an opportunity for true freedom.

This was an opportunity to free myself from the limiting beliefs that were holding me back. What are the limiting beliefs that are holding you back? Maybe you believe you're too old. Maybe you believe it's too late. Maybe you don't believe in you?

Free yourself from those thoughts that aren't serving you. You will feel like a huge weight has been lifted from your shoulders. These thoughts have been weighing you down as they were me. This was a chance to free myself from being a part of the status quo. This was a chance to go beyond a career that focused on my needs and wants, and become the servant leader I was destined to be.

TAKEAWAYS

For the first time in my life I saw how I could help others achieve success beyond their wildest dreams. I saw a way where common people with like-minded interests could lock arms and co-create something special, something that would last long after they were gone. This was a chance to create a true legacy. I was waking up!

What will your legacy be? When it's all said and done what will you be remembered for? As I ask you these questions, I do so because these were the questions I was asking myself. Change is difficult for everyone but necessary for anyone looking to move from where they are to where they want to go. Take a moment to reflect on your last 5 years. Take the space provided below and jot your routine for the week. Not including the weekends, is it the same, day in and day out? Are you truly happy or are you simply taking what the world has handed you? It's never too late to start dreaming again. Stay awoke my friends!

CHAPTER 8

NEW LIFE

*Have you ever felt
like you were meant
to do more than what
you are currently doing?*

You have this emptiness deep within knowing life at the present moment isn't quite where you want it to be. You want to do more, have more, and be more than you are, but simply can't seem to figure out your purpose. In the core of your soul you feel you were destined for greatness but feel like you're spinning your wheels getting nowhere. Join the club. I am here to tell you it does not' have to be this way.

Life is meant to be lived, yet so many will go to their graves having unfulfilled their dreams and destiny. I didn't want to be remembered for dope parties, club nights and as the late Notorious B.I.G. put it, "Party and bullshit!"

My goal in writing this book is to give you the motivation and tools to help you achieve my definition of true freedom. First freeing yourself from the limiting beliefs and second, freeing yourself from the self-doubt and undeserved self-scrutiny. Freeing you from protecting scarcity. So many people vehemently protect the very thing that has them stuck.

I need you to understand you have it within you to live the goals and dreams in your heart. My definition of true freedom is having options. Options create opportunities.

I realized that being Dj Finesse wasn't truly fulfilling and didn't match my definition of freedom. That career gave me "some" options but a lot of what I was doing seemed superficial.

Reflecting back on my time in the entertainment industry I now realize what attracted most people. People were interested in my success and how I was able to achieve it. Most wanted to know what it was like being "Diddy's Dj". I lost count how many times I was asked that question. Time after time I had to address their question and make sure the story was far from fabrication. For the record, I was an official Dj for Bad Boy Records NOT DIDDY HIMSELF!

I also realized most wanted nothing to do with Mason Santos. Dj Finesse was entertaining. Mason Santos wasn't interview worthy. I remember sitting with my boy Rich Dollaz in his condo in New Jersey. We were about to shoot a scene for VH1's Love and Hip Hop: New York, season four.

Rich and I met and became really cool after I finished shooting two shows on BET. He was one of the most prominent A&R's in the music industry working for Bad Boy Records. We broke a lot of Bad Boy Artist and did some amazing events together. I was asking him about being on the show on a more consistent basis and his response reflected my point.

I remember him telling me the producers of the show would have no interest in what Mason Santos cared about. Being a Behavior Specialist at a High School, being married, being a committed father and family man wasn't entertaining in the reality world space without drama. I realize now that what I cared for and my interests beyond music weren't interview worthy.

I wanted to be impactful. I wanted to make a difference. I felt getting people through the door of a club, into the VIP, or buying someone a drink was a hookup, not impact. I wanted to create something that impacted the masses. I wanted to know I had a hand in changing lives on a global scale.

Maybe this is you and you haven't found the vehicle to get you there. Follow your heart and trust the process you will find your calling. Just remember, it may not come in the package you designed.

What I have learned between the years of 2015 to 2020 has been a total eye opener. My goal is to open your eyes. I love it when I get a chance to hear my friend Max speak. One of his favorite lines as he is inspiring people from the stage is...

"Many people have sight but most lack vision."

There is a world out there beyond what you know to be true. There is a world I never knew existed. Many of us fail to see beyond the here and now. A lot of what I share in the later part of this book comes from my investment in personal development throughout these years.

As I continue to work on me, lessons continue to pour in. My mind continues to open. I chose to share them with you hoping some will resonate with you and help you achieve the goals and dreams in your heart. If one thing sticks with one person and helps them push through, this book is a success.

No matter the industry, understand success will never happen without sacrifice. I mentioned earlier that success will never bend to *no sacrifice*. There is no compromise. Sacrifice is simply part of the process. Sacrifice is to success as the tide is to the ocean. In other words, it's inevitable. Most fail to realize this and the result usually ends in futile attempts at something they thought they were interested in. Most won't go all in. Their attempt at success is mediocre at best.

> *If you are to be successful,*
> *hugely successful, I am going to*
> *prepare you for the inevitable.*
> *Success means moving from*
> *the old life to a new one.*

In order to create the new life you desire for yourself, you are going to have to detach from the old life. You are going to have to leave behind the people and things that aren't serving you. That may be one of the hardest things you will ever have to do.

As I stated previously, some of the people and things we love the most are the very people and things holding us back from greatness. How many of you reading this book have made an attempt to share something exciting with someone, and have gotten one of two responses. I don't have the money or I don't have the time.

Social media is amazing. People put their lives out for the world to see. The same people who say they don't have money always seem to find a way to spend the money they say they don't have.

The same is true for those who supposedly have no

time. You see them spending time in places that aren't serving them. None of what they are doing can move them any closer to their goals. Where are you spending your money and your time? Are you investing both in you, and your future?

If there's one thing I know for sure, people will find time and money for the things and people they feel are important. Having no money or time is relevant to the opportunity or situation.

You have to be able to show people true value. At the end of the day all people want to know is how will this benefit me? If you can show them a personal benefit, they will most certainly find the time and the money. This too I had to learn. Your willingness to learn and change is crucial to your success.

Change for most is extremely difficult because as humans we are creatures of habit. You will have to sever ties with limiting beliefs. What have you been telling yourself every day? What are you reading every day? What are you watching and listening to every day?

If we are
what we eat,
what are you
feeding your
brain?

> *The brain is the most powerful and important muscle in the body, yet the majority of people fail to nourish it.*

I was never a person to read so again this is a value I have learned later in life. I thought reading was boring and I was the type that needed to be doing something physical. I never found value in sitting still and being present in those moments.

Even in college I was never a reader. I truly don't remember reading anything from front to back. I was what they called a skimmer. I skimmed through books looking for the answers needed to do well on a homework assignment or test. Now things are different.

I have learned to enjoy reading books that help me to become a better person. I look forward to learning something new and gaining insight and different perspectives. After you finish with this book, I would urge you to continue to nourish your brain.

In order to do that, you are going to have to agree to continuous personal development. By no means am I saying I have it all together. Change was, and still is difficult for me. Change does not happen simply because you recognize some areas of your life that need improving. Change happens when you make a decision to do something about it and put a plan in action.

Today when it comes to my business, I am much more conscious of my surroundings and the people I associate with. I am constantly striving to be better and in order to do so I have to surround myself with people better than I. As a collegiate basketball player, I knew the more I played against the best players, the better I became. Success is the same.

Here's what's going to happen as you make the decision to cross over. I know this to be true for every single person I have come in contact with. As we've shared stories and testimonials, not one person reached the top of the mountain without sacrifice and pain.

The old life is going to rear its ugly head every chance it gets. Best believe when you start having success, old life is going to show up at your doorstep like a Jehovah's Witness on a Saturday morning. No disrespect to Jehovah's Witness, I just thought it was a good analogy.

Every time you are about to turn the corner, the old life is going to do everything in its power to keep you in that old space. The old life is going to act like a jealous ex-girlfriend or spouse. Not only have I heard the stories and watched others from my success team go through it, I have personally witnessed it in my own career. Let me share one of the most important stories in this book to illustrate my point.

One day I was sitting in an Arena in Las Vegas for a

conference with some of my success team. At the time of the event, I had been involved with my company for 2 years. I achieved a level of success fairly early. It took me 1 year to reach the level of a Director with the company.

As we sat and listened to each speaker, a common theme emerged. One, every person who told their story from the stage thanked God for their opportunity. Two, no matter where in the world they came from, their nationality or ethnic background, each of them went through some sort of pain or made an incredible sacrifice to reach the top.

The new life you want for yourself is the new relationship. It's something you are going to have to care for. You are going to have to focus and devote quality time to learning and studying. You are going to have to abstain from and identify the distractions that will present themselves with 100% certainty.

In order for you to succeed, it is going to have to be out with the old and in with the new. The new life is your new commitment. It, like any relationship is a roller coaster ride. It's never a straight road to the top.

There are going to be ups and downs. There are going to be times when the thrill of what you're working on takes your breath away. There are going to be times where the uncertainty creates anxiety. This is par for the course and true for any successful person. Success is hard work and those who have had to earn it will tell you the same.

I believe the life you want for yourself is within reach but not without a commitment. I was all in and I was committed to doing everything necessary to change my current situation.

As I sat and listened, I couldn't help but think there was no way I was going to reach the top without something happening. Who was I to believe I was special in that I would have a clear road to the top while everyone else had to sacrifice and go through the struggles that accompany success?

If you want to be successful, struggle is part of the process in any industry. You hear the cliché phrase no pain no gain mostly in sports but it's true no matter where you are in life.

> ### *Through struggle our character and resolve are tested.*

Going through the toughest of times is the test. How will you fare when you are tested? What grade would you give yourself as you look back on life's tests? *Remember there are no setbacks, just setups. There are no losses, just lessons. Everything you are going through now is to prepare you for the new life you say you want for yourself.*

I remember talking to my friend Stephanie who was sitting next to me in the conference. I mentioned to her what I was feeling because she had a very similar path of success.

I remember feeling there was no way I was getting up on that stage without some sort of struggle, some sort of pain. I knew I was going to have to endure something if I was to reach the level of success others were having. I needed a story and for the first time I knew Dj Finesse wasn't it.

All my accomplishments as Dj Finesse and playing college basketball opened so many doors but this was different. These were stories of true triumph. These were people whose faith and belief had been tested. I was witnessing what true courage looked like and I began to wonder if I was built for such a test.

Everything I had accomplished prior to this moment seemed inconsequential. Playing college basketball was never hard because playing basketball was a love of mine. Practicing never seemed like work for me.

Looking back, I can't ever remember a time where I felt playing basketball was a chore. Becoming a Dj was the same. I loved music and hip-hop so getting behind turntables wasn't work, it was a part of a culture I loved. Both basketball and spinning became default careers to one another. I was juggling two loves, and both were equally attractive.

This was a different feeling. This new life meant giving

up stuff. The biggest thing I had to give up was the old thinking. I had to embrace the idea of putting others first. This was about serving and leading people to their desired destination in life. Their wants and needs had to take precedence. This was no longer about me.

This was an area I had absolutely no expertise in. How do I lead people? What does true leadership look and feel like? As I continued to read and personally develop, I began to understand the importance of putting others first.

> *If you want to be*
> *successful in anything,*
> *know it is not about you.*
> *You can be good by*
> *yourself but in order to*
> *become great, you are*
> *going to have to commit*
> *to making everyone else*
> *around you better.*

I am not here to tell you who or what to believe, but I know being a servant leader is biblical. Service to many leads to greatness.

In order for this to happen for me the way it was happening for those individuals crossing the stage, I knew I was going to be tested, I just didn't know how. It was a bit nerve racking, but I felt I was ready to go through it if it meant leading from the front.

As you read this you might be saying to yourself, why would you put that energy into the universe? By all means I wasn't wishing anything bad on myself or anyone else, this was my humility kicking in. This was my realistic, honest observation of where I was in that moment.

Have you ever heard someone tell you to be careful what you ask for? Sometimes the biggest blessings will come from your biggest challenges. In order to be great, you are going to have to go through them. There is no way around them. This is where growth lives. Iron is shaped in fire.

In order to be successful, like a precious ore, you will have to be stripped down of who you are for who you want to become. Like ore going through the transformation process, the old you will have to be melted down. As you go through the fire understand the person that comes out on the other end will be an amazing new you worthy of greatness.

I have learned life is all about perspective. Your outlook on life and how you handle adversity says a lot about your character. As I begin to unpack this part of my life within these next pages, I truly believe I would not have taken the news the way I did if I had not been invested in personal development and if I had not found my calling.

What happened to me is the reason I began writing this book, so I want to be completely transparent and detailed as I write this. I believe God gives his biggest test to his strongest soldiers. My mother always told us God will never put more on you than you can bear and that was about to be tested.

I remember it like it was yesterday. My wife and I were vacationing in Mexico and towards the end of our stay I began aspirating after eating. It felt like the food was getting stuck in the middle of my chest. I found myself having to constantly clear my throat after eating certain foods.

At the time I didn't think anything of it. I assumed it was heartburn or indigestion. When we got home the issue continued and I decided it was time to see my primary physician. He suggested that I could be having an allergic reaction to specific foods and referred me to a dermatologist.

While there, they identified specific allergies and felt I needed monthly allergy shots. Mind you, I have never had food allergies in my life. So, I began getting monthly allergy shots. I asked doctors how long before my body would react to the shots.

I was told it would take 4-6 months before I'd see any real change. I decided after 4 months to stop. I had hay fever allergies when I was a teen but grew out of them as an adult. I knew in my gut this was a total waste of time and money. I felt no different after discontinuing with the allergy shots, so I knew once again my gut hadn't failed me.

In January of 2017 I was in Arizona for another

conference and became ill. At the time it felt like the flu. I treated it as such taking over the counter cold medicine and loading my body with Vitamin C.

After returning home to Rhode Island the fevers subsided and again it was business as usual.

Two months passed and it was now March 2017. The aspirating was still present but no worse than when it first began.

One day after showering I noticed a small lump on the left side of my neck about 4 inches below my jaw line. I made an appointment to see my primary care physician. As he observed the lump, he suggested it may be a swollen gland, and if it got any bigger I should come back. I kept an eye on it and a month later it was the size of a golf ball. I went back to see my primary care physician, and he immediately made a referral to Rhode Island hospital for me to have it biopsied.

Here is where I tell you that God works in mysterious ways. Again, this is not a book about my religious beliefs or my relationship with God.

This is my chance to tell you that for me, God is real.

I went to the hospital for my biopsy on a Monday. I was put under a local anesthetic and they used a large needle type instrument to secure a sample of the mass big enough to biopsy. I was told the results of my biopsy would be in within a few days. For me, I continued my day-to-day routine and kept plugging along. By Thursday of that week, I hadn't heard from the hospital.

At first, I felt no news was good news but as I looked at myself in the mirror each morning, I knew something wasn't right. Aside from this lump bulging out of my neck, I felt fine. I decided to call first thing Friday morning and got an answering machine. I left a message and a few hours later I received a return call with an appointment to see the doctor the following Monday morning.

As I arrived, I was a bit nervous but my need to know was much more important. As I sat with the doctor, he proceeded to tell me that they didn't get enough of the mass. I sat puzzled. I thought to myself, "seven whole days just to tell me you didn't get enough of the mass?" That to me was the first red flag. My Dj Finesse senses were ringing.

He laid out a plan that included cutting through the exterior of my neck to get to the mass and remove as much of the mass as he could. That was the second red flag! At that very moment my senses were on full alert and God went to work.

I have heard amazing stories of acts that only God could pull a person through. I have heard stories where people claim they heard the voice of God in a time of need.

I am not here to lay claims and say otherwise. I am not here to be the truth seeker for these people and their experiences.

What I can do is tell you how God showed up for me in my time of need.

As I sat with the doctor one on one, a feeling of calm came over me. There was no anxiety or nervousness as I asked the doctor a very specific question. At that very moment I asked the doctor if he were in my shoes, would he cut through his neck or go to Boston Massachusetts? I have to believe it was God that gave me the courage to ask that specific question. It was God that gave me the authority to advocate for myself.

In a moment where the doctor's pride and ego could have kicked in and lined his pockets with another surgery, God intervened. I mentioned earlier that people only know what they know. I have to believe that God gave the doctor the humility, integrity, and empathy to understand his own capabilities, and through this divine process, the doctor responded the way he did.

Of all the answers the doctor could have given, the doctor responded, "No, I wouldn't cut into my own neck." He told me he was fully capable of doing the procedure but if he were me, he would go to Massachusetts Eye and Ear because they are one of the best. It gave me relief to hear the doctor utter those words because at that moment I knew God had my back. That very day my wife and I made an appointment to go to Mass Eye and Ear.

Let me write this as a disclaimer. As a former college basketball player who loves the sport, it has always been my motto never to do anything to taint the game. With that being said, I have never done drugs or smoked cigarettes. I made it a point never to do anything that would cause irreversible damage to my body so that I could play as long as possible. Like most college students, I was a social drinker and tried marijuana a few times, but smoking wasn't, and to this day still isn't my thing.

The whole process to get to Mass Eye and Ear took close to a month, but I was confident I had made the right decision. My wife and I got in to see the doctor on a Thursday in mid-April. While there I explained the procedure Rhode Island Hospital suggested as a form of treatment and they immediately disagreed with their assessment.

The doctors told me they would go through my mouth into my throat with a camera and grab as much of the mass as they could. While under anesthesia they would biopsy the mass.

We scheduled an appointment for the following Monday morning. The biopsy took literally 30 minutes. When I came to, my wife and the nurses were standing by my side. They gave me some crackers and Ginger Ale to calm my stomach as we waited for the doctor.

When I heard those three words, "You have cancer," the first thing I felt was I had to be strong for my wife who was sitting beside me. As you read on, this sentence will be the last time you see the word "cancer" as I refuse to say the word and give it power! For the rest of this book and the rest of my life I will only refer to it as "C".

Little did I know my wife had already gotten the news? The doctor gave her the diagnosis from the biopsy while I was still under anesthesia. When she heard the words, he has "C", she told me she went into the bathroom and almost collapsed to the floor crying. I learned this only after I began to progress through my treatment.

How do you show up when you hear such unwanted news? Life is all about perspective. When I heard those words, I could have done one of two things: Give up or choose to turn my trial into triumph. My wife in the moment of despair chose triumph over trial.

I didn't know it but, in that moment, she was the epitome of strength and courage. She told me she had to hold it together and be strong for me. She knew that if I saw her as an emotional wreck, I would have known for certain it was bad news.

For those of you reading this who may be battling that awful disease or may know a family member, friend, colleague, or loved one battling this, or any awful disease, my prayers go out to each and every one of you. This chapter is your chapter of hope. Every last word I write is for you. Those three words or any other affliction does not have to be a death sentence. Not in its literal sense. It does not have to be the death of your dreams. It does not mean the death of your goals. Your diagnosis does not have to be your life's definition. I said in chapter 4 that life is 10 percent of what happens to us, and 90 percent is our response to what happens.

I had absolutely no control over what the doctor was going to tell me as I awoke from the anesthesia. He told me he had good news and bad news and like most, I chose to hear the bad news first.

I was diagnosed with Squamous Cell Carcinoma. My "C" came through the HPV virus. That was the bad news. The good news or silver lining was how the "C" responded to the combination of radiation and chemotherapy. The doctor told us because it came from a virus, that particular form of "C" responded extremely well to the combination of chemo and radiation. He added there was a 90% chance that it would never return.

As elated as I was to hear the news that this was a treatable "C" with a 90% success rate, I would still have to undergo chemo and radiation. As crazy as it may sound, after the initial shock, I didn't shed a tear. To this day I never have, and don't believe I ever will.

This has nothing to do with me being tough or men not crying and showing emotion. I heard something different when I heard those three words. I didn't ask why me? I didn't blame the world or claim I was dealt an unfair hand. Knowing how "C" has affected the lives of millions directly and indirectly, I or anyone else would be justified in feeling that way.

For me It was just the opposite. I knew I had been blessed with an amazing family and opportunities most will never have. I felt who was I to complain and doing so would be selfish.

As I processed what my next few months would look like a calm came over me. Two very distinct thoughts came to mind. I remember thinking of my new business endeavor. I began to identify with the amazing stories being told by all the people on stage. As weird as it may seem I knew at that moment I was going to hit the top of the company. I realized at that moment that this wasn't about DJ Finesse, the official Dj for Bad Boy Records. This was about Mason Santos the "C" survivor!

The second thought was extremely emotional. I stated before that the things you want and the life you desire may not come in the package you designed. I was gearing up for the biggest fight of my life! I had no idea how my body would respond to the treatment. All I knew was I had to fight. I had to fight because I knew others couldn't. I had to come out swinging for those who were ready to throw in the towel.

"C" has been the bully in the lives of so many and I knew I had to stick up for those who may have lost confidence and their will to fight. The feeling was indescribable but I knew in the core of my soul that I had to tell my story and do it in such a way that gave others the strength and courage to persevere and push through any obstacle standing in their way. I knew I had to win and the only way to do that was to proclaim victory.

I created daily affirmations I read each morning before leaving the house and again before going to bed. If you've never done affirmations before, below is the list I created for myself so you can get an understanding of the power of thought.

1. I am a survivor
2. I am "C" free
3. I beat "C"
4. I am strong
5. I am a winner
6. I am focused
7. I am determined
8. I fight for those who can't
9. My story saves lives
10. People fight because I fight

11. I lead from the front
12. I motivate the masses to continue to live and never give up
13. I am successful
14. I am wealthy
15. I help others create wealth
16. I am a go-getter
17. I attract other go-getters
18. I am a servant leader
19. God's got me
20. God is good all the time

I would strongly advise you to create a list of affirmations you read to yourself at least twice a day, once when you wake up and once before you go to bed. Your subconscious mind does not know the difference between reality and imagination. It acts upon what it sees and hears and accepts what it's being told. The more you introduce it to positive affirmations the more it will accept them as reality.

Have you ever heard a song on the radio that you absolutely despise and then a couple of weeks later you find yourself humming and singing along? The record labels and radio stations have affirmed that this is a song you should like.

The label floods the airwaves and you literally will

hear the song every 30 minutes. How many times have you changed the station just to hear the same song playing at the same time on a different station? You can't get away from the song. How powerful would it be to flood your brain's airwaves with affirmations and messages that actually serve you!

This was a complete shift in my thought process, and this has to be yours. The old life is going to throw everything at you to keep you connected to it. It's going to test every fiber in your body. It's just the way it is and to think otherwise is futile.

You are going to have to embrace the pain and use it as motivation.

After my diagnosis, I realized the life I wanted for myself changed *from personal to purpose*. I could see it as clear as day. I knew with complete certainty that God chose to use me. My victory is a victory for everyone. If you've gotten this far in the book, you've already won.

As you read this, I want you to take control over your life. I want you to understand that no matter what you are going through you can push through.

You are what you think, and we become our thoughts.

With that being said, every day I wake I thank God for giving me another day to inspire others to live. Each night before bed I ask God for the strength and courage to face life's challenges and be a living testimony for others. Through your story of success you are creating a narrative and blueprint for others to read and follow.

I want to take a moment and explain to you what my treatment looked like. I know it was far worse than some and far less invasive than others. Although I do not want your sympathy, I appreciate your empathy and prayers.

What I need from you at this very moment is for you to make a decision that nothing is going to stop you. To do that you MUST commit to helping everyone else achieve his or her goals and dreams! The shift in mindset from being served to being a servant leader is extremely difficult for most to do.

In our society most are taught to look out for themselves. I have learned that looking out for only yourself is a lonely road to nowhere. You might acquire a lot of stuff, but chances are you aren't fulfilled. As Tony Robbins says, "there is a huge difference between achievement and fulfillment."

How do you help others when you aren't where we want to be in life? How do you save someone from drowning when you're taking on water yourself you might ask? Here's what I know.

At some point in time you will have an opportunity to

do something good for someone else and you have to seize it. You may not think you have the ability to offer anything of value but trust me you will be throwing them a lifeline.

This book might be your lifeline disguised or wrapped in a different package than what you might have anticipated. Maybe one lesson or one story here will inspire you to act.

My treatment lasted 35 days. It consisted of 7 weeks of radiation, Monday through Friday, and chemo each Monday for 5 weeks. It didn't take long for the effects of the radiation and chemo to kick in. The first week was a piece of cake, as I felt no different.

I was advised that I should get a G Tube (feeding tube) and I remember being dead set against it. That was my PRIDE kicking in. I was adamant that I would get through the full 7 weeks without needing the tube. That was short lived.

I remember the day I realized I was losing my taste buds from the chemo. My friend Rob owned a new pizza shop and he brought some pizza to the house. As we ate, I couldn't help but notice the pizza was extremely bland and had a distinct metallic cardboard taste.

At the moment it hadn't occurred to me that my taste buds were dissipating. I not only told him the pizza was the worst I had ever tasted, I told him he should shut down his operation. My wife elbowed me and gave me that look with her eyes and eyebrows raised that suggested I be quiet and stop making an ass of myself.

I had no clue what she was talking about until she elbowed me again and pointed to my mouth. At that moment I knew things were about to change. I lost 8 pounds in week three alone and found myself in the doctor's office having a G Tube implanted in my stomach.

For the next 5 months all the nourishment I would need would have to flow through the feeding tube, this included all medications. Because of my inability to swallow, pills had to be crushed and flushed through the tube as well.

I had to force myself to take small sips of water and it had to be room temperature. The temperature of refrigerated water caused severe pain. The sips were just enough to exercise my throat muscles and keep them from atrophy.

For two weeks I had no voice. I remember trying to talk and no words or sound came out. The skin around my neck was bright pink as it burned from the inside out. I goggled with organic turmeric juice to help with healing and inflammation.

Oxycodone was prescribed for pain and anti-nausea medication to help with the effects of the chemo. Imagine the pain of vomiting when you have the equivalent of third degree burns in your throat. As if the feeling of being nauseous wasn't enough, the stomach acid from vomiting made the pain in my throat unbearable.

My saliva glands were burned from the radiation, so

my mouth was dry 24 hours a day. I found myself waking up at all times during the night with a need to gargle and rinse the dry mouth to avoid Thrush.

I took a medication to numb my throat so I could take my anti-nausea medication. In those 5 months I lost 46 pounds. If you saw me and didn't know what I was going through, there's no doubt from my appearance you knew something was physically wrong.

In the eyes of most, I had every right to shut down and isolate myself from the rest of the world. That was the furthest thing from my mind, as I knew I had work to do. Instead I chose to use social media as a tool to be transparent and vulnerable. I used Facebook as a platform to let people in and not push them away.

This was bigger than me and I knew this was my chance to tell my story. This was my opportunity to give others going through adversity strength and hope. I decided nothing would change. I was going to continue to be active and get out of the house as often as possible.

My wife came with me to my first two radiation treatments and I told her from that point on I was driving myself to and from each appointment and that is exactly what I did. I drove myself to all 35-radiation treatments and the 5-chemo treatments. I decided to get up and go fishing. I remember vomiting while fishing. I would grind my teeth and ball up my fists with anger like I was ready to fight.

Ironically, that is exactly what I was doing. I was fighting for everyone who lost his or her will to fight. I was fighting for anyone afflicted by this, or any other disease. I was fighting for families mourning the loss of a loved one. I was fighting for my family. I was fighting to create a story of strength others could use to push through. I was fighting and had no intention of losing.

The old life was throwing its biggest haymaker and if I could take this punch and do it publicly, maybe others would find the courage to stand up and go toe to toe with life's biggest obstacles.

What are you going through currently? What is the old life throwing at you? My hope for you is this book and the stories within can act as your corner man in your fight!

It had been three months since my last radiation treatment, and it was time to get a PET scan to see if the "C" was gone from my body. My wife and I went to Rhode Island Hospital on a Friday to have it done. After the scan was complete, they told us the results would be ready by Monday. As we pulled into the driveway, my wife stated she needed to run errands. I walked into the house, grabbed a blanket, turned on the television and hit the couch.

My wife couldn't have been gone 15 minutes when this feeling came over me. At that very moment I felt amazing! I felt a sudden energy rush and I looked around puzzled. My eyes, forehead and eyebrows were squinted trying to understand what was going on?

All of a sudden I felt like I needed to hear music. This is the God's honest truth! I jumped up from the couch and ran into my Dj room. Everything was disassembled, as I had not spun in months. Quickly I assembled my equipment, turned everything on and began spinning as if I were in a club. The music was blaring, and I could not help but dance and sing!

I immersed myself in the music and got lost in the moment. I truly do not know how long I was spinning and didn't hear my wife come in. She startled me as she was standing in the doorway. She had this blank stare on her face as if she had just lost her best friend. I smiled at her as I turned the music down and asked her what was wrong. She said nothing.

I walked up to her and asked her again what was wrong, and I began to see her eyes tear up. She reached out to me and as we embraced she told me I did not have "C!" As I glanced over at the clock it had been a few hours since she left to run errands and I asked her, *how she knew?* I remember saying to her, *I thought they were supposed to call on Monday?* She smiled as a tear ran down her face and said they tried calling me, but I didn't pick up, so they called her with good news.

As we hugged all I could say was, "I already knew it!" She asked me how and I told her the feeling that came over me when she left. I mentioned to her the feeling that came over me was not just any feeling. That feeling was God! Again, I am not here writing this to tell you who or what to believe in. I can only tell you my story as real and as transparent as I can. This is not doctored up for your entertainment. This is for you to use however you see fit.

For me, I did not hear God's voice. He didn't speak to me or command me to do something in particular. I felt his presence and love. I felt he knew I had passed the test. In my darkest hour he saw me stand for others. He heard me reach out to him. He saw me put others' needs first in a time where I would have been justified in being selfish.

I have to believe God felt I was ready to lead the masses. I had to be battle tested if I were to lead others out of darkness, out from fear, out from their limiting beliefs, and out from a life of mediocrity.

As I continue on this journey, I give God all the glory for my new life. Where I am today and my approach to life is nothing short of amazing! I am a Behavior Specialist at our local high school adding value to the lives of hundreds of students.

I have been invited by the head basketball coach to teach basketball skills development with our Varsity and Junior Varsity teams. My Dj career is flourishing. I am having huge success in my Network Marketing business. If you are reading this, I have become a bestselling author!

My relationships with my wife, kids, family, friends, and colleagues couldn't be better!

My intentions are clear and my goal for you is clear. The feeling you will feel when you make a decision to move on from the old life to the new life will be like a weight has been lifted off of your shoulders. The air will smell fresher, the food tastes better. You will sleep better as you are stress free. You will see and respond to people differently. Take my story and use it to understand the concept of being a servant leader. Remember to always put the needs of others first.

Be mindful in your words and truthful in your actions.

Move with integrity, honesty, and humility. Lastly, be truly interested in others success and grateful for the opportunity to help them achieve it. When you do this, give God the glory! I promise you, you are sure to close the chapter on the old life like I am closing this chapter of this book.

TAKEAWAYS

I really want you to dig deep. Turning the corner in life is not going to be easy. I believe there are a lot of amazing lessons, and true personal experiences that will help you move forward.

Here's your homework for this chapter. I've provided 2 columns on the next page. On the left side, label it "Goals and Dreams." Create a list of ALL the goals and dreams you've ever had. In the second column on the right, label it "Obstacles". Create a list of everything and everyone standing in the way of those goals and dreams. The right column is the old life. You are going to have to address those issues on the right side if you want to move to the new life. Finding the inner strength and courage to address the issues on the right column is the start of The New Life. In that process I hope you find your true calling. It will not be easy but trust me it will be worth it!

Goals and Dreams	Obstacles

Goals and Dreams	*Obstacles*

CHAPTER 9

BUY IN
VS.
BOUGHT IN

You can bring a horse to water, but you cannot make them drink. At some point in your personal life or business career, I am sure you've heard that statement. Maybe it was said to you or you might have thought it was fitting to say it to someone else. Maybe it has come up in casual conversation. Nevertheless, I wanted to dissect that statement because it may make the difference in your business if you can grasp what I am about to say in this chapter.

As you read this chapter you will notice references related to Network Marketing or Multi-Level Marketing (MLM). I don't want to lose you so please read this paragraph before skipping over to the next chapter.

Many of you reading this may have no interest in MLM or have never been a part of a Network Marketing company. I am a part of MLM, and I absolutely love everything about my company! First let me make perfectly clear this is NOT a chapter written in an attempt to recruit anyone into my business. You will see I have purposely left out my company name and platform. If you truly have an interest in what I do related to MLM, you can go to my website or follow on social media, and I'd be more than happy to share it with you.

My goal in writing this chapter is to offer professional advice for business owners or soon to be business owners. I am not here to convince anyone that MLM is in your best interest. I am here to tell you that *Buying In is!*

Buying in means committing to personal development.

I was driving in my car one day and I began thinking about my business in Network Marketing and MLM as a whole. I often drive in silence. Concepts seem to flow when driving and when I wake early in the morning.

I was trying to wrap my head around why so many people join Network Marketing companies but most fail to take meaningful action? I think it's important to give you a little history on the industry of Network Marketing. The first Network Marketing Company was started in 1932. As an industry, MLM goes back almost one hundred years so the answer to why people jump in and take no action couldn't be the industry.

The OG's of the Network Marketing industry - Tupperware, Amway and Avon - are household names and have been so since as early as the 1940's. MLM as a whole has created more millionaires than any other industry in the history of business itself. So why do so many quit?

Although what I am about to say is directly related to those of you involved in Network Marketing, the principles in this chapter can be applied to any industry or occupation. First, let me say that I am not a Network Marketing guru. I haven't spent enough time in the industry to hold that title.

Conversely, I have been involved in MLM long enough to recognize the issues that keep others from taking meaningful action. I have suffered from some of the same issues and this is why I am confident in writing this. Here is what I know. I know no matter the industry, you need to become fluent in that industry's language. You need to immerse yourself and study the industry you intend on working in.

I am a lifelong student of learning and you should be as well. I recognize that success in any industry is a process and a journey. If you are to be truly successful, you are going to have to become a lifelong learner and a student of your industry and company.

As the leader of a large growing team, I see so many issues that affect so many people in Network Marketing. I want to dissect a few of them here for you. Know the issues I discuss here have absolutely nothing to do with the industry. I am not here to say the industry is perfect, no industry is.

I was asked once about the pros and cons of Network Marketing. As I thought about the question, I knew my answer would be ambiguous, as every person has had a different experience. For me, the pros of MLM are the different people you meet along your journey. The ability to meet and connect with people from all walks of life from all over the globe is amazing.

Having the ability to meet complete strangers and find the common thread that binds all of you brings me gratification. Strangers can become family. The ability to witness and take part in the personal, professional, and financial growth of each person you touch continues to be a humbling experience. If you are truly invested in others success, the feeling you get when you see lives transform in front of you is incredible!

Obviously, the wealth you can create for your family and future generations goes without say, but I am not driven by money. I am driven by a thirst to see you grow, develop, improve, and succeed. If money is your driving force go with grace but be careful. I have seen what the love of money can do to relationships. People who chase money tend not to be loyal to anything or anyone, and they will often do anything to anyone to get it.

I was then asked what I believed was the downside to Network Marketing and I responded - *the people!* People can be both the gift and the curse in MLM! As gratifying as it is to see people winning in all facets of their lives, it drives me crazy watching people settle for mediocrity.

It is extremely hard for a person like me to accept. As a leader and mentor, you constantly look for the good in everyone you meet and lock arms with. You often see more in people than they see in themselves. I have had times where I felt I wanted success for them more than they wanted it for themselves. I see this across the board: Men, women, young and old, white, or black.

As a leader it is your job to motivate, encourage and compliment, but know you cannot push a person in a direction they don't wish to go.

My goal is to meet you where you are in life and in business. My intention is to help you transition from good to great. As with anything in life none of what I am saying will work if you aren't honest with yourself. It won't matter how many times you reference these chapters or any other book you read. It won't matter what audios you listen to if you are not real with yourself about where you are in life, your business, and why you're stuck.

In Network Marketing I have come to know people who have far more experience in the industry than me. I am more than fortunate to call many of them mentors. I would not be where I am today without their continued support and guidance. I have learned a great deal and I am a sponge whenever I am in their presence. For that reason, I am able to talk to you in this manner.

So why is it so many join network marketing companies and fail to take action? Why do so many jump in and quit at the first sign of trouble? How is it that so many get on board with an exuberance for change and an excitement for their future just to see that sparkle in their eyes diminish soon after they join?

During the first few years of building my network marketing business I would rack my brain over this question! I began thinking about the statement in the very first sentence of this chapter: *You can bring a horse to water but you cannot make them drink.* I started giving that statement some real thought and it hit me.

No matter what you do and how much attention you pay to detail, some horses will never drink. No matter how much you try to motivate and move people to action, some horses will never drink. No matter how good the opportunity or how amazing the product is, some horses will never drink. No matter how amazing the compensation plan is or how amazing the training and support systems are, some horses will never drink! The quicker you realize this, the better off you will be. You will have to get over the emotion of it all because some of these horses will be your family, friends, and colleagues.

I remember the feeling when I started with the company I am in now. My thought was, leave no man behind. That soon became exhausting. My shoulders are broad but carrying people became emotionally draining.

Byron Schrag is an amazing talent in MLM. The moment you hear him speak on stage you will understand within seconds how special he is! He has reached the top of our company not once but twice.

He is one of the most sought-after trainers not just with our company, but also in MLM. He trains nationally and internationally and has one the largest and fastest growing teams in MLM. He has hundreds of thousands of customers spanning the globe so to say he knows what he is talking about is an understatement. He is one of the most charismatic and energetic trainers and pulls no punches. When he talks, I make it a point to listen.

I remember asking him a building question and how to better inspire, motivate and lead my team. I did not know it but each person I was carrying and caring for was becoming a burden. The load was becoming heavier and my business was not growing nearly as fast as I'd liked. He made a couple of statements that put the first point of this chapter in perspective.

He told me, *"You can't push a dead bear up a tree."* Some people in your business are going to be dead weight.

They will jump in and tell you their plans to "crush it." They will tell you they have scores of people lined up ready to join. Sure enough, their words and actions look incredibly different.

You start to notice their communication becomes less and less. They stop returning text and phone calls. You look in your back office and you notice their account is inactive for non-payment or they've resigned with absolutely no notice. Sound familiar yet? It's par for the course and trying to change that behavior is like pushing a dead bear up a tree.

I have seen Byron train on several occasions and when this topic arises, the message is the same. *"It's much easier to give birth than to try to resurrect the dead."* Go find new people who want change and help them attain it.

> *Realize you can't save everyone and it's not your job to do so. It's your job to know what you have your hands on, know it adds value, share what you're excited about, collect a decision, and be the best leader you can be.*

Those willing to drink will, and others simply won't. If you're in MLM and want to win big, you are going to have to detach the emotion from the outcome. I see so many people take it personally when they share their product or opportunity and are met with a "no." They act as if the person just broke up with them.

I have witnessed people quit after their first "no." I continue to sit in disbelief wondering who the hell would allow someone else to have so much power over his or her future. This was one of the biggest inner battles I had to grapple with. You will have to understand when they opt out, they aren't quitting on you, they're quitting on themselves or their future.

Think of it this way. Have you ever gone out to dinner? I am going to assume everyone reading this book has. Let's look at the dining experience through the eyes of a waitress. If she is really good, the relationship starts with the introduction. She approaches your table with a smile, energy, personality, and confidence. After all, she's done this hundreds of times.

She proceeds to address the table and first offers to get everyone beverages. She wants to be efficient but does not want to rush the dinner experience. She returns with drinks and if she's really good, some bread and allows the table to engage in small talk. She returns and begins to go over the day's specials. After a few moments of letting you all ponder your meal choices, she asks if the table is ready to order. She places the order and the food comes out in a timely fashion. The smell is as tantalizing as is the presentation. The food is amazing, and the portion size is more than you can handle. You eat as much of it as you can and decide to take the rest home. The majority of the table is as stuffed as you are.

The waitress checks on the table from time to time making sure everyone is enjoying their food and if she can, offers anything else the table may need. The food and service are amazing and right when you think the dinner is complete, here is where the sell for dessert comes in.

She is following a simple system. The waitress comes to the table and asks the question they are trained to ask everyone. Yes, you guessed it; "Can I interest you in dessert?" You're thinking to yourself there's no way you can eat another bite, so you respond with a polite "no, thank you," as 90% of people eating out do. The majority of the table does the same but there is always one person who orders desert.

Here is where I want to make the point about detaching from the outcome and having "buy" in. The waitress knows 90% of patrons won't order dessert but she asks the question anyway. She does not flinch because she knows it's not personal. She understands the table isn't saying no to her, the table is saying no to dessert. This is the same in your business.

When people choose not to buy your product or service for whatever reason, they aren't saying no to you personally. They are saying no to your product, opportunity, or themselves. Imagine if every time she was told "no," she became emotional. Imagine if she started becoming discouraged, and emotional each time she asked patrons if they wanted dessert and was told no? What if she started making statements like, "This waitress thing doesn't work!" Or, "No one wants to order dessert from me, so I think this is not for me." What about the people who tell her, her offering dessert is a scam? If she took it personally and internalized the responses, she would never be able to waitress anywhere.

Conversely, your waitress knows as long as she follows the system, and sticks to her training, at some point the "no's" will become "yes". While everyone is sitting back stuffed, the waitress engages in a conversation with your friend about dessert and what happens next is masterful.

For the lesson I am trying to share, and make it easier to follow along, I'm going to use my friend Chris. Chris is from Chicago. We met in college, and to this day he is one of my best friends. Chris is part of the 10% who always orders dessert! This is what I have noticed the really good waitresses do. They offer Chris the dessert menu and after he orders, the waitress disappears into the kitchen. Her return to the table is amazing! Every time I go out to dinner I look to see if the process from waitress to waitress is the same.

With the dessert on full display for everyone else to see,

she does not go straight to Chris. She makes sure she takes the long route around the table so all of you who said no can get a glimpse of what you turned down. Chris on the other hand is focused. He could care less what the rest of the table does, nor should you in your business. Chris and the waitress have already cleared a landing space for his dessert.

At this point, all eyes at the table are on the waitress swooping in with Chris' dessert. When it hits the table, it's not long before you and everyone else has his or her eyes on the dish. Chris begins to indulge and as sure as the night is dark, three questions that are sure to be asked, fly out of the mouths of everyone else. *What did you order? Is it good? Can I have a bite?*

Every time this happens, I just smile and shake my head. All of a sudden, you're not so full anymore. You signal to the waitress and you ask, "Can I have what he's having?" Every time this happens it drives the point home that you have to have "buy" in. You have to understand and respect the process of getting someone to buy, whether it's desert or any product or service. People telling you "no" is a part of the growing process in MLM and any business.

With any transaction of goods and services, people are going to make decisions they believe best serves them. If you show them real value, in their mind you've justified why it makes sense for them to spend their money.

Good waitresses are invested in the process of going

through to "no's". They keep in perspective that their job is to present patrons with food options, become the best server they can be, collect a decision, and detach the emotion from the outcome. If you can detach the emotion from the outcome and follow a simple system, you will be much more successful not only in MLM, but in business in general.

Looking back on my start with the company I am with now, I realize I had bought in financially, but I hadn't bought in to the idea, the company, and the product. I was new and I was in Dj Finesse mode. In my first three weeks I jumped in and did everything wrong. I truly felt my name alone was all I needed to get my business off the ground. I was that guy saying I am going to crush this! I started verbally explaining everything to everyone and I was told no by everyone. They didn't want dinner, bread, drinks, dessert, nothing!

Three weeks in and my initial excitement was gone! Sound familiar for any of you trying to build your MLM business? I was like the rapper Drake who created a song called "In My Feelings" and boy was I caught in my feelings. If I was a waitress, I had no business waiting tables.

I remember telling my friend who sponsored me I was quitting. Can you guess my reasoning? I told him this thing doesn't work. How many of you have been building your business having major success and have had a new person tell you the business or opportunity does not work? I know what you're thinking, *the nerve of some people!*

I am sure that's exactly what Max was thinking about me. Now I understand the value of buying in or being vested. If you find the right company with the right product and leadership, the system is set up for you to win if you follow it. My friend Max has an amazing acronym for the word system. It stands for:

<u>S</u>ave
<u>Y</u>ourself
<u>S</u>tress
<u>T</u>ime
<u>E</u>nergy
<u>M</u>oney

I had no buy in so of course I wasn't following the system and I began playing the blame game. It was the company's fault I wasn't winning right? After all, I was Dj Finesse! I had high credibility and I had been successful so if people weren't joining, it had to be because of the company and the product. It couldn't possibly be me?

I paid my money to join but I wasn't being coachable, and I was about to receive a huge wake up call. I mentioned earlier that life does not give you what you want; it gives you "who" you are. I was hungry for success and my life's waitress delivered me my dessert. She brought me a huge piece of humble pie! Trust me it wasn't easy to swallow.

Humble pie has a horrible taste in the beginning but once you own it, you'll find the taste is unbelievably delicious!

> *How many of you*
> *are willing to let*
> *go of who you are*
> *for who you want*
> *to become?*

How many of you are ready to buy in and be coachable? Too many of you are living in the past as I was. You aren't ready to let go of the things that aren't serving you now. They may have served you in the past, but you are attempting to write a new chapter.

Who you were and what you've done may not necessarily transfer to where you are now and where you say you want to go. You are going to have to learn new skills for your new industry. Out with the old and in with the new.

I started to realize the majority of people in my business were buying in financially but very few were making the commitment to buy in emotionally. The majority lacked conviction. Are you seeing this in your businesses? Chances are you see and have witnessed exactly what I am talking about. Why? It's human nature.

We are born to win but programmed to lose.

Every one of you reading this was born with greatness inside of you. You were born to have more, be more and do more. You weren't designed for mediocrity. At some point in time you decided to give up on your dreams. You decided the effort you needed to put in to win was too much to ask so you settled.

How many of you thought you would be further along in life at this stage?

Too many people aren't willing to sacrifice to get where they want to be. Instant gratification is running rampant. This is the, "What can you do for me generation."

I was taught if you give a man a fish he will eat for today, but if you teach a man to fish, he will eat for the rest of his life. Unfortunately, most want to be fed. Most are not willing to go through the process of baiting the hook, and fishing for success. They want the fish to jump into the boat. That's what was happening in my business.

I was growing a team of people waiting to be fed. Most would not do for themselves, and I happily obliged. If this is happening in your business I have the answer! In comes life's waitress with my second piece of humble pie. Look in the mirror! As I mentioned earlier in this book...

The answers to most of life's problems lie in the mirror.

Too many people blame their lack of success on everything and everyone else. Quitting for so many seems to be the easiest option. I know because I was ready to do the same. I literally told my friend who sponsored me that I was out. Because he joined three weeks prior to myself, he wasn't able to help get me off the ledge. Instead he told me I should speak with our up line. Thank God it was Max.

I met Max at the Marriott in Providence, Rhode Island and he asked me what was going on. I remember telling him I was out. He asked me why I was quitting, and I told him I didn't believe this thing worked. Mind you, here I was three weeks in, telling my up line who had been in the company 2 ½ years having massive success that this does not work?

He asked what I was saying to the people I was approaching, and I began to rattle off words. I specifically remember him putting up one finger at a time for each word I used he knew would make people run for cover. After he had a fist full of no-no words, he stopped me dead in my tracks. What are the MLM no-no words you might ask? Here is the list I gave Max in our conversation that I would advise you to remove from your invite, and the psychology behind them. When you use these words, this is what people hear.

Presentation: They will think they have to sit for hours and people feel they are too busy and don't have time. They won't show!

Opportunity: They will think most opportunities are too good to be true. Sounds sales pitchy and they won't show!

Meeting: People don't want to sit with a bunch of strangers. It tends to feel like an intervention. They won't show!

Money: The number one of the no-no words. They know it takes money to make money and most feel they don't have any discretionary income to blow or invest. When people hear, "We can make money," they wonder if it's trustworthy and they won't show!

Your Product: Remember people are creatures of habit and product brand loyal. They will automatically feel you are discrediting their brands. You've also given away the plot to your movie, so they feel they have enough information and they won't show!

Business: Most people already work too much. The idea of working more and having another boss sends them running. They won't show!

Network Marketing: Most people's default response is Pyramid Scheme, Scam, Ponzi Scheme or, "it's one of them things." They definitely won't show unless it's someone who has MLM experience.

Max understood I was super excited about the company. When he stopped me from rambling he proceeded to ask me two questions. The first question he asked was if I was willing to be coachable? I told him I was. Max had what I wanted so I ate my slab of humble pie and listened.

The second question was the most important and I want to make sure you understand this point. He said to me and I quote, "Finesse, I know you can say what I am going to tell you to say, my question is WILL you say exactly what I am going to tell you to say?"

If I am being honest, I was a bit reluctant and a bit hesitant, but I had this gut feeling he was telling the truth.

Again, he had the results I wanted. He told me all he wanted me to say to everyone I knew was, "I got something you gotta see!" I looked at him with a puzzled, confused look that suggested I thought he was out of his mind. I told him there was no way that was going to work.

I felt people needed more information in order to show up. He stopped me and repeated, his second question. "WILL you say what I am telling you to say?" I sat still for a few seconds as he awaited my response. I told him I would say exactly what he suggested I should. In the next 3 weeks, I signed up 6 people and the rest is history.

What I realized was my own stunning observation and I wish to share it with you now. I want you to really think about your business and level of leadership as I ask you this question. Before I do let me reiterate that some horses no matter what you do, will refuse to drink.

We've established that, but can it be that the horse isn't drinking because it knows you aren't drinking?

Think about that for a moment. The horse is looking at you and it's going to do what you do, not what you say. That's basic human behavior. It sees you aren't committed to the water, so it's not committing.

You aren't excited about the product or opportunity, so your people aren't excited about the product or opportunity. If you aren't committed to the process and journey, chances are, they aren't committing to the process and journey. If your team sees you getting emotional, you've now taught them how to respond when times get tough. Your lack of interest to personally develop is apparent so you need to attend training and invest in yourself if you want them to do the same. If your lack of buy in is what drinking the water represents, why the hell would anyone drink the water?

Would you follow you?

Would you join your team? So many people say yes to that question and they are not being honest with themselves. In the beginning of my MLM career I wouldn't follow me, nor would I join my team. I wasn't ready to lead, and I wasn't excited about the products or opportunity. I had no idea what training and personal development looked like.

People will continue to make a financial investment, but it does not necessarily mean they are ready to commit to investing in themselves, and their future. You have to lead them. You have to be committed to drinking the water! It can't be phony enthusiasm. People will see right through the bullshit. You have to buy in totally if you want others to do the same.

Take this story and the lesson behind it. Life is a culmination of choices. You can choose to do things your way and continue getting the same results. If your way is truly working, kudos to you and continue to crush your goals. If not, I would advise you to humble yourself as I did. Decide that being coachable is in your best interest because being coachable is buying in.

> *Buying in is deciding to*
> *fight for your future and*
> *not buying in is the same*
> *as deciding to quit on it.*

If you chose to not buy in, it's only a matter of time before you quit. It takes no more energy and no more thought to quit. I am telling you it's time to decide to man or woman up and face you. It's time to hold you accountable.

> *Why is it easier to expect*
> *more from everyone else,*
> *than you do yourself?*

To me that's a cop out! It's time to stop pointing the finger at everyone else and hold yourself accountable. I know this may sound a bit harsh, but you will thank me for it later. Becoming successful is worth it but no one ever said it was an easy road to travel.

We all have defining moments. I believe if you've gotten this far in my book, this is one of them. This is the moment you chose greatness over mediocrity. This is the moment you say enough is enough and you let go of the past and focus on the future. This is the moment you decide there is no benefit in not buying in!

If you do, I promise life will look different one year from now. This will be the moment when your business starts to flourish, and life starts to take on a whole new look. It begins with you buying in and being totally transparent with yourself.

None of what I say is fiction. This is all real life and real stories intended to help you push through. I started looking at myself. I saw the issue and it was literally staring me in the face. I was enabling my people. My business wasn't growing because I wasn't growing. I realized I had to become the person I was looking for. I had to be the person I was trying to attract. Your business is only going to go as far as your personal development will allow it to go.

I began thinking of all the conversations I was having with my team. Start thinking about the conversations you are having with yours. Think about what needs to change in order for your business to go to the next level. It's you! You are going to have to buy in if you want to go to the next level. Remember, people aren't buying the product or the opportunity. They are buying you! If you're not fully committed to drinking the water, the horse won't be either!

TAKEAWAYS

This chapter has a lot of references to Network Marketing or Multi-Level Marketing (MLM). Think about your approach to your MLM or business. How you do something is how you do everything! Look back at some of the projects or businesses you've started and never finished. Ask yourself, did you go ALL IN? Were you committed to finishing or conveniently giving yourself reasons to justify your quitting? Has not finishing become your legacy thus far? Again, be honest with yourself in the space provided below. Look back at what you wrote and identify if the problem is the horse, or who is leading the horse?

CHAPTER 10

PURPOSE FULFILLED

We've come to the end. Before I conclude I want to thank God for this amazing opportunity. Without his grace none of this would be possible. I do not say that lightly. God has been good to me since he showed up in my life in 2017. I genuinely want to thank each and every one of you who took the time to read this book. Although I am the author, this is your book. It was written with you in mind.

I hope you found and continue to find value from the lessons inside. I hope it becomes a piece of work you can reference time and time again when times get tough. When you need motivation to help you push through. When you are leading teams in your prospective industries. When you may be on a plateau in your businesses. Or strictly for entertainment purposes.

I hope the lessons become a part of your daily routine.

I want to thank everyone who referred this book to their friends, family, and colleagues. This has been an amazing journey. Every story, every account, every word has been carefully thought out. Everything you've read is real and came from a place of love. I want you to be better because you deserve it. If no one has told you, let me remind you how special you are.

Let me conclude by saying this. Although I am not a huge fan of football, I am a fan of the drama the sport creates. For the record, being from New England, I am a fan of success and the Patriots have more than proven they have a winning system that is immensely successful.

A lot can be learned by watching their approach to winning. Their attention to detail, sacrifice, and how they demand excellence and buy in from every player, has created one of most dynamic dynasties of any sport in any generation. Consider their approach as a team and an organization and relate it to where you are in your life and business.

Do you demand excellence in yourself? Do you pay attention to the small details? Are you willing to sacrifice who you are for who you want to become? Will you commit yourself to buying in completely?

I want to use a football analogy for the last lesson. Let's consider the Two Minute Drill in football. For non-football lovers, the Two Minute Drill is a drill team's practice when the game is on the line and down to the wire.

Teams literally put two minutes on the clock and practice the need to score under pressure conditions with limited time to do so. With that being said I have always wondered about the psychology behind the two-minute drill in football and why teams consistently practice it? Some might say it's the ability to deliver under pressure and push through adversity. Others might say it teaches a winner's mindset, teaching players to understand that as long as there's time on the clock, you still have a fighting chance. All true I might add.

The question I have is why do teams practice a sense of urgency for two minutes and not the entire game? I have always wondered why so many teams fail to execute, or move the ball and score until it's absolutely necessary. I wonder how teams and players would perform if they approached all 48 minutes like they do the two-minute drill?

As I began conceptualizing the Two-Minute Drill as a whole, and how it relates to success or the lack thereof, I started questioning why so many people coast through life? Why do so many coast in their approach to success, goals, and dreams?

What would your life look like if you approached everything the same way football teams approach the two-minute drill? Do you think you might be further in life than where you are today? If you answered "yes," ask yourself why are you coasting? Where is the sense of urgency?

We allow life to beat us down until we feel the walls closing in and then we act out of a sense of desperation. It does not have to be this way. I am here to tell you don't have to be in pain to act with a sense of urgency. The wheels don't have to fall off in order for you to feel you need change. Change can happen in a time of bliss as well. If you want different options for your life all you have to do is make a conscious decision to change, take action, and do it with urgency.

One of the toughest things you are going to have to do if you want to be successful is address the past that may no longer be serving you. I mentioned in chapter one how breaking my family's cycle was vital in my process of moving from where I was to where I wanted to go. Who you are and what you've done up to this point can't get you to where you want to go.

One of the biggest mistakes you can make along your journey is thinking everything and everyone around you has to change. If you are to be successful, you are going to have to change. Change means learning new skills and personally developing. I was never a person who read books. Now I read 10 pages a day, I listen to audio and I attend personal development conferences. The better you become, the better equipped you are to handle what life throws at you. Remember, in chapter four I mentioned life is 10 percent of what happens to us, and 90 percent how we respond to what happens.

People are creatures of habit so understand your changing will be a process. We only know what we know, and we don't know what we don't know. How we approach life is all learned behavior.

From the time we were children, our environment acted as our training facility. We modeled the behaviors and the people we saw on a consistent basis. It became our reality. As we move through life, we reflect on prior knowledge to help us make decisions we believe will serve us in the moment and in the future.

Some decisions pan out and others not so well. It's part of life's course as we continue to learn lessons along the way. Some lessons sting more than others but remember, if you learn from lessons there are no losses. One of the biggest lessons I had to learn was the importance of needing to know more than I knew if I wanted to become better in all aspects of my life.

I remember when my daughter was thirteen trying to figure out life. For any parent reading this, do you remember when your child became a teen? They thought they knew it all and you knew nothing, right? It was like we had never been through anything and every answer we gave was the wrong one.

I remember having a conversation with my daughter

and I told her, figuratively, that she didn't have to run into the wall headfirst to know it's going to hurt. She was making decisions we knew would have negative repercussions. But as most do, they go sprinting past you headfirst into the wall, and of course, it hurts.

Although you the reader may not be a teen, as people we often sprint headfirst without mapping out the path before us. That approach to life can be costly. Too often people act without planning. I am not here telling you what to do. That is not my place. This book was intended to be a blueprint of sorts. A guideline you can follow to help you get beyond your current state of mind. The intent was to offer you a different perspective and help you realize you don't have to put yourself in harm's way in order to change.

This is your life and you are going to live it your way. What I know is I am blessed to have met people along the way who took a genuine interest in my interests. I was humbled by my failures. Those failures and experiences allowed me to open up to people who helped me not only understand the importance of growth, but also gave me confidence that I could achieve a life beyond my wildest dreams.

Like the story of the king, every now and then we all need a push. We all need guidance. We all need a mentor, a coach, or a friend that sees more in us than we see in ourselves. We need that person who can deliver the message different from the voice we hear in our heads daily.

The voice in your head is like your favorite song. You know the melody and every word because you play it over and over every day without fail. You've cemented the message deep into your psyche and now it's time for a new song. It's time for a brainwash. It's time you wash your brain of all negativity and all the lyrics to your song that isn't serving you.

I believe everything I went through happened for a reason. All the good and all the bad is a matter of perspective. Everything you are going through is happening for a reason and now you are here at this point in your life.

I hope you have a different perspective that will allow you to approach life's challenges differently than what you were used to. Remember two plus two is four and it will never be anything else. Change creates change so how will you respond and how will you show up? What will you do differently? I hope you know you deserve to be happy. You were born to win but programmed to lose. Not anymore! Like children who grow out of their old clothes, it's time you grow out of all the old habits that are holding you back from greatness!

I hope this book has been an eye-opener for you just as it has been for me. Writing this has allowed me to look back on my life and connect the dots. Writing this has been a humbling experience to say the least.

I have tried to be as transparent as possible in an attempt to connect with each and every one of you. The stories have always been a major part of who I am, but the lessons came later. What is your story and what lessons have you learned? How will you connect the dots from your past so you can continue to move forward?

Now is the time, or as my mentor Dave Ulloa states, "When would now be a good time to start?" As I mentioned in this book, procrastination is the cousin of mediocrity and there is no benefit in waiting to live the life you were designed to live.

Like the surfer's mindset, I hope this book not only allows you to recognize opportunities before they arise, I hope it gives you the courage to start new ventures as well. I hope it gives you the confidence to start that business you've always wanted to start or take the dream vacation you've always wanted to take.

I hope this book inspires you to start checking off the bucket list items now rather than later. You've got one life to live and tomorrow is not promised to any of us. Every moment is a gift so what will you do with the time God gives you? Treat every day you wake like a reset button. It's a new day to first be thankful, and second, each new day is another chance to go after your goals and dreams.

Before I conclude, I don't know what year it will be when you finish reading this. I started writing this book in

2019 and finished in February 2020. On January 26, 2020, the world was shocked to learn that one of the greatest basketball players of all time lost his life in a horrific helicopter crash.

Kobe Bryant was 41 when he passed. The world continues to mourn in disbelief. As if losing Kobe wasn't bad enough, the world had to come to grips with knowing his 13-year-old daughter Gianna and 7 others were also killed in the crash. I want to send my deepest condolences and prayers to the families, friends and loved ones of Kobe and Gianna Bryant, Baseball coach John Altobelli, his wife Keri and their daughter Alyssa; mother and daughter Sarah and Payton Chester; Mamba Academy basketball coach Christina Mauser; and pilot Ara Zobayan.

Please take a moment from reading this and hold someone close to you tight. Tell him or her how much you love and appreciate them. No one is promised the next minute. This tragedy has opened the eyes of a lot of people. All too often we come together in death or when a tragedy happens. We should come together, as we are all human and in need of love, affection, understanding, solace, sympathy, and empathy. Here is my plea to you. We don't have to lose a loved one for us to be better to one another.

A tragedy does not have to happen for us to put the needs of others before our own. I want to end this book with what may be the most important and significant lesson. It's the lesson of TIME.

Have you ever wondered why everywhere you go, everywhere you look there's some sort of device that tells us the time? Time is everywhere. You see it on the walls, on the stove, on your microwave, on your cable box or smart television, on the dashboard of your vehicle, on your wrist, or on your computers, tablets, and phones.

It's because time is the most precious commodity and these instruments are constant reminders. Time is the one thing that cannot be bought, and it cannot be sold. It's seldom used wisely, and all too often taken for granted. It's the one thing every single person on this planet wastes, and when time isn't on their side, wishes they had more of.

Time is the one gift given to you that you cannot re-gift. When it's gone, it's gone. So, my question to you is what will you do with the gift of *TIME*? Do you understand it's a gift? Do you understand its value? If you knew you were running out of time or had very little left, would you approach life differently? See this isn't about you or me. This is a message from me to you, about you and me, and the time we think we have that we really don't.

The problem with people and time is too many walk-through life as if they have an abundance of it. We do it unconsciously every day. Every time, (ironically) we make statements like, "I'll do it later," or "As soon as I get this or that, then I'll do it," or the worst of them all, "I'll get to it tomorrow." I believe we are subconsciously playing God.

Only the Almighty knows if, "Later" or "Tomorrow" will actually come for any of us. Yet, so many of us conveniently make these statements.

It's time that allows us to do something, or nothing at all but understand either way, whether you choose activity or inactivity, you are using it. The question is are you using it wisely or wasting it? Are you wasting time going to a job you hate? Are you wasting TIME in a dead-end relationship because you don't value yourself enough and your time? Are you wasting time on things and people that one, can't give you a positive return for the time you've invested, and two, don't deserve your time?

If you understand how TIME works then you know none of us are promised another second. At any moment everything we know can be gone. In a second, we can cease to exist. I know this because my diagnosis told me so. When I was diagnosed with "C" it put my time here on this earth in perspective. I realized in an instant the importance of the next second, the next minute, the next hour, the next day, month, and next year.

Here's my suggestion to everyone reading this: Let today be the day you begin valuing your time completely! Today's the day you make a decision to stop throwing your time in the trash like unwanted food and place it on the mantle where it belongs.

Cherish it, savor it, honor it because today is the day you decide to spend time with the people you love doing the things that make you happy. Today is the day you say to yourself I am not going to waste another second on anything or anyone that isn't adding value to my life.

When it's all said and done and you look back on your life, the biggest question you will have to come to terms with is...

What did I do with my time?

Did I live or just exist?

Did I accomplish the goals and dreams I set out to accomplish or did I squander opportunity after opportunity by wasting time?

There are plenty of things we will take to our graves; let's make sure regret is not one of them. In those last few moments, as you look back on the time you were given here on this Earth, will you be able to say you did it all? Can you say you were time wise? I read a quote once that said...

> *"At the end of it all you*
> *will be more disappointed*
> *by the things you didn't*
> *do than by the things*
> *you did do."*

Everything you didn't do does not have to be your legacy especially if you are taking the time to read this. This is your wake-up call. This is your life's alarm clock ringing in your ears. This is your time and you don't have it to waste, so go do something with it and turn your Personal into Purpose!

TAKEAWAYS

Here is where you reflect on how this book helped you as a whole. Remember learning is a lifelong journey and as I move forward as a writer, it's important for me to be open to all feedback. Summarize how this book made you feel while you were reading it. What emotion did it stir up? Is this a book you feel you will hold on to for future references? Lastly, I would love to hear from you! Shoot me an email and let me know the changes you've made and how this book helped you with your breakthrough. What does life look like now? I will do my absolute best to respond to EVERY person who took time and embarked on this journey with me, I am forever grateful! May God bless you all!

Go Turn Your Personal into Purpose!

Sincerely,

Mason S. Santos

Thee Dj Finesse